LIFE AND TIMES OF AN AMBASSADOR
AND 15 SEPTEMBER, 1958

Toki Matsudaira

LIFE AND TIMES OF AN AMBASSADOR, no. 1
AND 15 SEPTEMBER, 1958
Copyright © Toki Matsudaira 2008

All rights reserved.

ISBN 978-184426-491-5

First Published 2008 by
UPFRONT PUBLISHING LTD
Peterborough, England.

Printed by Lightning Source

About the Author

Toki Matsudaira who is the author of the book, was born in 1944 in Tokyo, Japan at the Red Cross Hospital. She was educated in the Sacred Heart School in Albany, New York, and then embarked on a one year study at the French Lycee in Manhattan in 1961. Her immediate and famous novelist writer relation of the family was Yukio Mishima, and many years ago, the more famous Lady Murasaki, who wrote "The Tale of Genji", a story of Court Life in 16th century Japan.

The biography speaks of her father Dr Koto Matsudaira, whose career as Japan's leading diplomat serving in the Gaimusho, is well recorded in as far as the work he contributed outside his own country of Japan, in the years 1955-1965. He retired in 1965.

Married and divorced, with two children, Toki Matsudaira has lived in London, England since 1969. She studied at a tutorial college for young ladies in Oxford, England from 1963-1965. Trained as a fashion model at Lucy Clayton, London. Did a secretarial course in London, and worked for various art galleries between 1967 - 1969, including Marlborough Fine Art Gallery and the Royal Academy .

August 29, 2007
Synopsis for "Life and Times of an Ambassador"

Dr Koto Matsudaira was from Japan, born in February 1903.Having trained at the Peers School and continued on to University where he studied his doctorate of law and international law, he went into the Foreign Office and served as a career diplomat throughout, until his retirement in about 1966.

He went through two World Wars and served at the League of Nations twice in Geneva Switzerland. He opened the doors of Asia for trade with the West and signed the San Francisco Treaty in 1956.

His career saw him going off to such distant shores as Paris, France, Washington DC, Russia, where he was interned during the Second World War, Canada, New York at the United Nations and New Delhi,India.

His daughter, Toki, was born just weeks before he was assigned to Russia, and in a train journey which lasted weeks, (Trans Siberian Railroad) the mother father and myself, Toki-chan, arrived in a country which could boast food availablility to eat and drink so different from a losing and war torn Japan unable to find hardly anything at all in the way of food subsidies. When Russia joined the War, we were interned in the Embassy compound hardly able to leave.

This is like an adventure story, but the difference is that it was our life story enacted as if it would last forever.

I have tried to put in only the more amusing aspects of his career and of his life as both a diplomat and as my Daddy.

It was the better part of my life in many ways, and my fond memories survive to tell the reader a life of legendary people and their times in the fabulous 1950s and 1960s. He could hardly be considered in present day terms anything other than completely glamorous! He would be amused to hear this if he had stayed alive.

This is a collection of memoirs which I have drawn up ,which can only illustrate the distinguished diplomat he was at the time of the United Nations before he was reassigned to India. It was his meeting at the Security Council with Cabot Lodge which started his career as a prominent one, when he agreed with the American that there should be a withdrawal of American troops from Lebanon where a local conflict had erupted. My father suggested that the U.N. should have a peace keeping force, and one which could offer U.N. Policing. This shot him to remarkable futures for the United Nations Peace Corps which until then only offered U.N. observation teams abroad. However it took Japan a long time to decide in favor of my father's idea. It was not until recently 2005 that Japan offered military aid in war zones such as in Iraq The "cheque book "policy was noted as a failure on the part of the Japanese government in response to and in the place of meeting military aid and humanitarian relief programs for the defence for the U.N. in areas of the world at war. However, this is much in the minds of most nations now, to receive that cheque and that pay to counter measures against terrorism and their wars and other requisites by nations which often admit their distance from a peace aligned program such as countries who participated with Adolf Hitler in the Second World

War.

The ways of diplomacy are not discussed as a main prerogative of this book apart from the letters and speeches my father made in his time in Canada and at the United Nations. It was a fine occasion when he met the Vice Chancellor of India to present his credentials as the Japanese Ambassador, "extraordinary and plenipotentiary."

His life and times both official and private are described vividly and without much difficulty. I hope the reader can learn something about the life of a career diplomat with it's ups and downs it's highs and it's lows. His service will not be easily forgotten by many who may prefer to remember him. Always a good friend, he left many who mourned his death when he died in May 1994.

I write this for my children and grandchildren as well and mark a special note here to say this.

Tokiko Matsudaira
03/04/08

LIFE AND TIMES OF AN AMBASSADOR AND 15 SEPTEMBER, 1958

Toki Matsudaira

My father was His Excellency, the late Ambassador, Koto Matsudaira, of Japan to Canada, the United Nations in New York, and New Delhi, India. He started his life in Tokyo, born 5 February 1903. (photo) He attended the Peers School. He usually walked all the way from his house in Denenchofu to his school everyday, some ten miles through all weather conditions, and was told by his father that it would make a strong man out of him.

Later he passed the Diplomatic Service Exam of Japan in 1926, a year later graduated from the Faculty of French law of Tokyo University, then studied in France and took his Doctor of Law Degree at the University of Paris, France.

He was an Attache at the Embassy in France in 1931 attended two League of Nations meetings in Geneva and 1934-1941 was with the Ministry of Foreign Affairs, Tokyo.

My father was posted to Washington as First Secretary of the Japanese Embassy only a few months before Pearl Harbour. He was interned there until the exchange of diplomats was arranged in June 1942.

After serving again in Japan, he was posted to Moscow in 1944 when I was born. We left for Russia, when I was exactly one month old! However no sooner had we arrived there then Russia joined the War and declared War against Japan in 1945 and for the second time, he was interned. My Mother and I, as a small baby were also interned!

I was born in August 1944, Tokiko Matsudaira, Toki being my nickname. My mother was Ai, my father was Koto. My parents were Japanese. My grand-parents lived in Tokyo, in a residential area in a house designed by Frank Lloyd Wright. Although I was a war baby, I survived and live to write this book, many years later, in London, England, where I have lived and married, and agree I am very far away from my home and my country. However, I still visit Japan, and enjoy my visits there, when I am able to go at all.

Now I will begin my biography of my father as well as some life history about myself, during and after his life, recording much work he helped the U.N. with when he was posted in New York as Japanese Ambassador. His influence in diplomacy during his time as a career diplomat working for Japan is what has impressed me, the most.

Photo of me as a baby. I look heavier here than my father who looks as if he could do with some food

When we were moved to Leningrad in 1944 or early 1945 , we were forced to stay in our compound and my father recounted a story about white Russians trying to flee the country, very impoverished and seeking both a job and shelter. They worked at the Embassy and eventually the Embassy granted them travel papers to leave. I think they paid this by giving over their jewels. The night before or a few days before they were due to depart in secrecy, they were found hanged in the downstairs basement of the enclave, and the horror that my father felt was enough to make him remember this story which he did tell us like repeating and going over a terrible nightmare he never quite forgot. He continued saying that after this incident, none of the Embassy staff dared to leave the compound, and only when it was absolutely necessary to do so. They realized they were being watched by the KGB although they were diplomatically immune! I think my father learned a thing or two during his Russian days about communists and the reality of living behind the Iron Curtain rather than the free world he knew so much better and obviously enjoyed. I will now write down the explanation of communism.

COMMUNISM: A theory of society according to which all property should be vested in the community and labour organized for the common benefit.

2) Any practise which carries out this theory

3) In these curious creatures, communism prevails to it's fullest extent, one for all and all for one.

JG WOODHOU.S.E.

COMMUNIST; An adherent of the theory of communism. attr. The communist doctrine of not paying a man in proportion to his work.

Hence communistic (in both senses)
What then is the reverse of communism? I will now write down the dictionary's explanation of capitalism.

CAPITALISM: The condition of possessing capital or using it for production, a system of society based on this; dominance of private capitalists.

CAPITALIST ; one who has capital especially one who uses it in business enterprises (on a larger scale)

CAPITALIZE;...3) To compute or capitalize the present values of 1856. 2) The project of capitalizing incomes 1856. Hence capitalization.

In New York, before I came to London I remember how New York remembered their Russians. There is the famous "Russian Tea Room "in Manhattan. I'm not sure when this Tea-Room was created, but it is a place to meet with friends for coffee, lunch, tea or dinner and used a lot for pre-theatre engagements and especially for going to Carnegie Hall, nearby. Many Russians came to Manhattan after the Russian Revolution, if they could escape Russia. It is one of the most famous land-marks in Manhattan which makes room for the free-loving Russian. It was a time, when I was still very young I met Mardi Hughes who introduced me to a Russian Prince who was then a student at University. He was related to Mardi, who was a great friend of my father and a reputed hostess. It was the period of the great Elsa Maxwell "the hostess with the mostest" as she was referred to in society.

Following a further period of service with the Gaimusho or Foreign Affairs Ministry, he was appointed Ambassador to Canada. He arrived there in early 1954. I was just a young girl at a Convent Boarding school in Albany New York. I will later explain more about myself and how I ended up in the United States. My father arrived just in time in 1954 to sign a new trade treaty between "our two great nations". I quote now much of a text of a speech my father made, on 14th April 1955 in Canada which was presided by the Chairman a President Mr James H Joyce. It starts:

MR JOYCE; We are glad to welcome as our speaker today His Excellency the Honourable Dr koto Matsudaira, the Ambassador of Japan to Canada, who will speak to us on "Japan's Position in the Far East"....

DR MATSUDAIRA; I consider it a great honour indeed to have been given the privilege of addressing the members of this Club today, because I am well aware of the contribution of your organization in furthering the better and fairer understanding of international affairs, in which, I should like to say, Canada is playing an ever more important part.

I should also like to mention what an honour it is for me to represent my country in Canada.

I understand that you would like to know something about the position of Japan in the Far East today. Before entering into a discussion of this problem, I imagine that it would not be out of place to give you a brief historical background of my country.

In July, 1853, Commodore Perry, commanding four United States' ships, steamed into Tokyo Bay with his fleet of "black ships" as they were called by the Japanese of that day, and opened Japan for trade with the West.

A feudal and medieval Japan thus found herself thrown into a world in which world-wide politics were rife and the struggle for colonial possessions was going on. In the

Asiatic mainland was a powerful Chinese Empire, Tsarist Russia was a mighty force in the north. Japan was faced with the necessity of building up her political and economic strength without delay, or else submitting to foreign pressure. Her young, patriotic leaders, therefore , were determined to create a modern Japan , a major power which was to become a worthy member of the family of nations.

The speed with which Japan was transformed into a great , industrial power in just three-quarters of a century can still be regarded as an extraordinary achievement. Western culture, science, industrial techniques and thought took firm roots in a virgin soil. Parliament of government was established. Japan fought two great wars and emerged victorious. In World War 1 she was a staunch partner of the Allies.

Thus, in the early 1930s, and in the course of some fifty years, Japan built an Empire, became a world power, signed the treaty of Versaille as one of the principal allied and associated powers, and was an original member of the League of Nations. Her Empire was prosperous and powerful. Her position as the stabilizing force in the Far East was secure. Then came the day of disaster, revealing to the proud how the day of doom, which may lurk in the destiny of nations and men, can be so close to the day of glory.

Now in what position did Japan find herself when the Last Great War ended? She had lost forty-five percent of her territory and twenty-five percent of her national wealth. Hundreds of cities were razed and millions of homes were destroyed. Her prosperous colonies and Empire were gone, and her once great merchant fleet no longer existed. And in the same breath, she lost her traditional markets, as well as her important sources of raw materials.

Now I would like to say a few words about Japan since the war-what her position is in the present state of affairs. I hope that these few words will help you to understand – even in a small and hurried way the problem of present-day Japan.

Many of you probably noticed the results of the recent general election held in Japan. This election was watched with particular interest by the rest of the world because it gave an indication of the future course of the Japanese people. More than seventy-five percent of those eligible to vote cast their ballots. Out of four hundred and sixty-seven seats in the House of Representatives, the Democrats, who form one of the conservative political parties of Prime Minister Hatoyama, won one hundred and eighty-five. The liberals, another conservative party, won one hundred and twelve votes. Together they control an absolute majority in the House. The Communists, who at one time after the war had thirty-five seats, put up seventy-two candidates and only two of them were returned. Their defeat is significant. The Socialists won one hundred and sixty-six seats.

In 1946, thirty-nine women were elected to the House of Representative has dropped to around three per cent, a figure which I would like to emphasize. Economic reforms have also been instituted. The former powerful Zaibatsu combines have been dissolved. Anti-monopoly legislation has been enacted. Sweeping land reforms have been successfully carried out. At the end of the war, fifty-four percent of the land was owner-cultivated and forty-six percent tenant cultivated. At the end of 1950, the percentage of the former had risen to eighty-nine percent and that of the latter had dropped to eleven percent.

After all I have said, I think I should not define the whole problem. What is wrong with Japan? What is the trouble that besets her? What is the difficulty which her leaders must face and tackle without delay?

Japan's fundamental problem is one of population. In an area a little more than two-fifths the size of the Province of Ontario or one-fourth the size of the province of Quebec live some eighty-six million Japanese. This is the equivalent of more than six times the population of Canada, In Canada you have a density of population of 3. 65 persons per square mile. In Japan it is 620 persons per square mile. But far more important is the figure in terms of arable land, 3, 422 persons per square mile, the highest in the world! If you had the same density as Japan, you would have an almost unbelievable population-a figure that I think will shock you-two billion, two hundred and sixty-eight million! This is just about the population of the entire world today.

Now, every day, Japan has three thousand new mouths to feed, every month ninety thousand new babies, every year one million more in population, the size of the population of Toronto! At the present rate, Japan's population will reach one hundred million by 1970. Emigration will not help very much. The present plan of the Japanese Foreign Office is to arrange for the emigration of 50, 000 in 1956 to the Latin-American countries: the figure for 1954 was 3, 500.

We are faced, therefore, with the necessity of finding some means to support our population, that is to say, to maintain and improve the general standard of living and to find new jobs for the riding labour force. We cannot do so with the resources within our own borders. Every bit of arable land in Japan is so intensely cultivated that the meager soil will produce, per acre, 1. 6 times more than that of the United States. But still we are dependent upon imports for about twenty per cent of our minimum food requirements. That represents $600 million in terms of money, or , in other words, half of our export revenue, The only answer , as I see it, is to develop our foreign trade to the utmost in order to earn foreign exchange with which to purchase the food we need. Our industries must be revived and strengthened. There is no country in the world today for which international trade means life or death to such an acute extent than Japan - not even Great Britain.

Since the end of the war, we have been at grips with this difficult problem. The task is not an easy one. The problem has been made even harder by the high cost of production. Our labour costs are no longer low, as they were reputed to be before the war. The whole result is one of impressive instability in our trade balance . In 1952, the deficit in our trade balance amounted to $750 million, in 1953 to $1100 million and in 1954, $1100million. The deficit was alleviated by off-shore procurement; but now with the Korean War at an end, we can hardly expect to rely on that indefinitely. You might see how precarious is this situation. Nevertheless, a slight improvement is being made and the Finance Ministry was able to announce during the last few days that the foreign exchange balance for 1954 was $344 million in credit. Japan's foreign exchange reserves were $977 million as of December 31, 1953, and $1. 180 million as of March 31, 1955.

Let us look for a moment at the trade between Canada and Japan. You may be aware that Japan now ranks as Canada's third best customer-exceeded only by the United States and the United Kingdom-and as Canada's second best customer as far as wheat is concerned. This year we are spending more than one hundred million dollars in Canada the majority for wheat, barley and pulp. In 1953, we sold in this country goods to the value of approximately thirteen million dollars, while our purchases from you totaled close to one hundred and two million dollars.

It is our utmost desire to continue and to expand, as far as possible, our growing trade with Canada, for we are convinced that, in this way, not only can we complement the eneds of another, but, also, through fair and honest trade, build up and deepen the good understanding between our two peoples. However, I might venture to say, that it is difficult to see how such a one-sided balance can continue indefinitely.

Perhaps the strongest argument for increased and balanced trade between our two countries is that it would be to our mutual benefit, in the long run. It is only through mutually profitable trade that we can improve our respective standards of living. The woodsman in British Colombia, the farmer in Manitoba, depend on a balanced and long enduring system of trade between us to maintain and improve their individual, personal well-being. By buying more from Japan, you are ensuring the welfare and happiness of their children and of themselves.

It is time now to examine the position of Japan in East Asia. Before the war, and taking the 1934-36 average figures, Japan depended in China to supply 68% of her coal, 36% of her iron ore and 40% of her industrial salt. Japan's exports to China, Korea, Formosa and other neighbouring countries amounted during the same period to an average of 42 percent of our total annual exports. This has not dropped to 9 per cent of the total in pre-war years, have now increased to 36 per cent. You will understand how Japan's economy, now depends on her trade with Southeast Asia and on the possibilities of its expansion!

If Southeast Asia should go Communist, Japan will not be able to stand alone economically. The fate of Southeast

Asia is therefore an object of real and grave concern to us. The political stability and economic development of Southeast Asia, on the other hand, will greatly strengthen Japan politically and economically.

Economics represent a vital element in determining the political future of Southeast Asia. If China under Communist control makes rapid economic progress, leaving the comparatively slow Southeast Asian countries far behind, there will develop a great margin between economic standards in Communist and non-Communist areas of Asia, enabling Communist China to place the whole of Southeast Asia under her influence without resort to arms.

The present per capita national income of Communist China, with a population of 580 million, is estimated to be approximately $50. A similar index for Southeast Asian countries, with a population of 620 million, stands at nearly the same level. (That for Japan was $170 in 1953, still 20% per cent lower than the pre-war level.) Therefore, we may assume that Communist China and Southeast Asia are on an almost equal level at present. The political future of Asia will be acutely influenced by the extent to which either of these two areas surpasses the other in the attainment of a higher national income.

The scale of capital investment is often a decisive factor in determining the rate of economic development. By our calculation, the funds necessary to execute the now contemplated development plans by the Governments of Southeast Asian countries reach a total of $9.28 billion. It is expected that 37 per cent of the amount will be furnished by foreign investors. The amount of investment per year will be $1.67 billion-$2.6 per capita in relation to the population. On the other hand, total investments made in

new cook was in her opinion, better suited to cooking for many people and even for banquets. He was a local cook, who was the cook of her first husband's cousin, then the Chilean Ambassador to India. She acquired his cook as he had been reposted to Yugoslavia, and no longer employed in India. My step-mother had in fact acquired a very fine cook who knew how to prepare just about everything possible. He was a wonder. In the beginning of our stay in New Delhi, I rarely saw Shuichi , as there were many more servants working at the residence then we had ever employed before. The cook and his family eventually returned to Japan, and I must say I never saw them again.

New York
September 15, 1958
Gaimusho, Tokyo

"Your Excellency,

I have the honour by direction of the Minister for Foreign Affairs, to declare on behalf of the Government of Japan that, in conformity with paragraph 2 of Article 36 of the Statute of the International Court of Justice, Japan recognizes as compulsory ipso facto and without special agreement, in relation to any other State accepting the same obligation and on condition of reciprocity, the jurisdiction of the International Court of Justice, over all disputes which arise on and after the date of the present declaration with regard to situations or facts subsequent to the same date and which are not settled by other means of peaceful settlement.

This declaration does not apply to disputes which the parties thereto have agreed or shall agree to refer for final and binding decision to arbitration or judicial settlement. This declaration shall remain in force for a period of five years and thereafter until it may be terminated by a written notice. "

I have the honour to be, with the highest consideration,
Your Excellency's obedient Servant.
Koto Matsudaira
Permanent Representative of Japan to the United Nations

My father's popularity and importance shone through over a question of Lebanon where a local war had erupted . Here I will explain from an excerpt called "Rocky Road".

"…The U.N. corridors and lounges on Manhattan's East River reflected a gathering tension. The Iraqi delegate, whom the Soviet Union tried unsuccessfully to unseat, remained at his post, lonely and forlorn, ignored by most of his fellow Arabs. Ironically, the nation that had butchered Budapest and flagrantly violated the will of the U.N. now posed as the champion of small and weak nations invaded by foreign troops.

The U.S. case itself was pockmarked with the legalisms in which the U.N. delights. Before the Iraqi coup, the U.S. had been determined to stay out of Lebanon, even greeted with relief the findings of the U.N. observers and the possibility of some domestic compromise. Now in the face of U.N. reports that no conclusive evidence existed of massive infiltration, the marines had landed.

"The Sole Purpose…" At the start, Henry Cabot Lodge was painfully on the defensive. He began with a bit of dramatics, which, as things turned out, proved unfortunate, by reporting the murder of the Iraq's former Prime Minister and the U.N. Delegate Fadhil Jamali. "Only a few weeks ago he was here with us. We heard his voice. We rejoiced in his humour. Now we learn that he was not only murdered but that his body was actually dragged through the streets of Baghdad. " Then doggedly, but with difficulty, Lodge tried to get around the touchy point that the U.N. was already on the scene in Lebanon. He praised the work of the U.N. observers , while at the same time, declaring them inadequate to fulfill their mission. The presence of U.S. troops, he said, "is designed for the sole purpose of helping the government of Lebanon, at its request, in its efforts to stabilize the situation, brought on by the threats from outside. "The U.S. would move out just as soon as the U.N. troops moved in. "

Shrewd poker faced Arkady Sobolev of the Soviet Union blustered that the whole U. S, position was "insolvent". The troop landings, he pointed out, had come not as a result of anything that had happened inside Lebanon, but were triggered by the coup in Iraq. The U.S. action, therefore, was a gross intervention into the domestic affairs of the states in the area. Sobolev demanded the immediate withdrawal of the marines.

The argument was a sharp one, but far more damaging to U.S. prestige was the position of Secretary General Dag Hammarskjold. Plainly miffed at the implicit U.S. flouting of the U.N. observers, he pronounced the observers' operation a "complete success. "

"Into the Wastebasket". On the second day, Sobolev made the most of the Secretary General's position. The U.S. , he said, had thrown the work of the U.N. "into the wastebasket" while still singing eulogies to the group". Under the circumstances said he piously, no self-respecting state in Asia or Africa or Europe for that matter, will agree to send troops to pursue the purposes which the American troops are supposed to seek in Lebanon". What was the U.S. doing but resorting to Hitler's "big lie"? retorts the U.S.'s Lodge acidly. I must defer to Mr Sobolev in the knowledge of Adolf Hitler, because his government was once an ally of Adolf Hitler.

Up to that point, the debate had been for the most part one between the two old adversaries. But now, meticulous, bespectacled Koto Matsudaira of Japan spoke up for the first time to express his government's misgivings" over the U.S. intervention, and said that he would try to seek some sort of compromise. To add to the U.S. discomfiture, bald Omar Loutfi of the United Arab Republic produced a letter from the president of the Lebanese Parliament denouncing U.S. intervention as an infringement of Lebanese sovereignty. Finally, as the second day ended, still another sour note was sounded. Gunnar Jarring of Sweden showing the irritation of his countryman Hammarskjold declared that in view of the American landings, the U. N observer should be withdrawn. In effect, this would mean that the U.S. would be left to get out of its predicament as best it could.

"When the Patient is sick". By the time the Council reconvened, the British had landed in Jordan. Taking the offensive, Lodge endorsed the British decision, went on to regret the Swedish position. "When the Patient is sick", he said, is no time for the doctor to leave. " He insisted that the U.N. observers had not been able to get behind all the rebel lines, cited U.S. evidence of infiltration, added that the shrill incitements of Cairo newspapers and radio alone constitutes interference. "Is United Nations to condone indirect aggression in plain clothes from outside a country? " If it cannot deal with such aggression, said Lodge, leaning forward intently, "the United Nations will break up. "

Sobolev dismissed the U.S. evidence as mere hearsay, - idna baba skazala ("an old woman said…") Before voting on the Russian, U.S. and Swedish resolutions began, he jubilantly declared that if his own was defeated, he would call for an emergency session of the General Assembly. Then, using Russia's 84th veto, he killed off the U.S. resolution calling for a U.N. force. Only he and Sweden voted for the Swedish resolution, only he for his own. At this point the delegate from Japan, worried about the U.S. position, got ready his compromise. He proposed the creation of a larger and really effective U.N. team, which would permit the U.S. position, got ready his compromise. He proposed the creation of a larger and really effective U.N. team, which would permit the U.S. to withdraw its troops with some assurance that the independence and integrity of Lebanon would be preserved. If the Russians were concerned about getting U.S. troops withdrawn , they could hardly object. But who could say that this was what the Russians were really interested in?

You may wonder what is the United Nations and what is their purpose? The United nations is a body of countries forming a membership at the United Nations building in New york or Geneva, where they discuss ways of instituting international security and peace, and uses itself for this purpose.

It does not necessarily mean that they are always fair and equal in their voting system, which delegates can revoke by a veto.

If we look back at history, we are told that the world system was established under the Treaty of Westphalia in 1684, I quote from a passage written by Murata Koji who explains it this way: The Treaty of Westphalia of 1684 "drew a sharp distinction between the anarchy that would reign among those states in international society that lack strong sovereign government and the hierarchy of domestic society in which a government exercises ultimate power. But this distinction was not strictly observed as international law and organizations were established and ultimate authority, even in domestic society, was not always unilateral. Then, in the latter half of the twentieth century, as interdependence among nations deepened, ties between international and domestic politics grew increasingly strong. This phenomenon came to be described as "intermestic", a term coined in the 1970s by combining the words international and domestic. "

According to Article 51 of the United Nations Charter, the right of individual or collective self-defense is an inherent right of member countries. When in July 1958, Japan joined the United Nations, U.N. Secretary General Dag Hammarskjold called on the Japanese government to send SDF personnel to join a U.N. observer group. In response, U.N. Ambassador Koto Matsudaira made a controversial comment in the Yomiuri Shimbun newspaper: "Some people in Japan advocate the strengthening of U.N. diplomacy, but from my experience I believe that what other countries in the world want Japan to do is to send SDF units to serve in the Congo (and elsewhere) as part of U.N. forces. Under the Constitution the dispatch of troops overseas is considered impossible, but SDF personnel should be sent at least as observer. I believe that in the future (SDF personnel) should be part of a U.N. police force as well". "U.N. Ambassador Matsudaira's statement that the basic way of cooperating with the United Nations is to join the U.N. police force is mistaken. " (Tanaka 1997, 210-211)

The 1990s saw the crisis in the Persian Gulf and the imminent war in Iraq. These were challenges to international security. The Government of Japan tried to pass a U.N. Peace Cooperation Bill, but it failed to pass the Diet. In spite of their reliance on Middle eastern oil and backing from the United States, Japan could not cooperate in the transportation of supplies, and was only able to give financial assistance. Japan contributed $13billion but it was hardly appreciated and called at the time their "cheque book policy". By the time Japan was ready to involve itself in the Gulf war by sending in minesweepers the Gulf War was already ended! "

During the 1950s JAPAN's ideological view of war were reduced to only two types of war: "wars of aggression and wars of self defence".

However the Gulf War was neither a war of aggression nor a war of self defence. Japan did not recognize the matter was one of international security which she failed to respond to promptly enough.

My father's understanding of military intervention in Lebanon siding with the American Cabot Lodge was the beginning of many meetings and discussions related to military intervention, policing and military policing as exercised during the time of the 9/11 attack in Manhattan. There have been wars in Yugoslavia, East Timor, Afghanistan, Iraq as well as the humanitarian crisis facing such countries as those mentioned in Africa and many more facing homelessness and migration throughout the Middle East and Africa. There have been endless refugee states and wars against them. The Governments have all learned to resign themselves to the international state of anti terrorism and it's laws by now. All the policing and all the military be they American or U.N. speak of the intolerable difficulties besetting various communities since the entre of their drugs and it's wars.

This is the worst war of all, in my opinion. The latest fad is drugged meat. I could die for it and also be put into a tin to be fed to the cat! This is the new terror wave of the new condition of their war and their want for drugs and it's human meat or flesh! There is no qualification needed for this war. Anyone can join in. Therein lies the nature of the terror and their secrecy and their secret conspiracies. It takes a lot more than that to overcome them and it is no matter to resign oneself to belonging to their secret society or become unto oneself an official for unless one has that insight into their war their side to be bugged or eavesdropped, one will be sprung a terrible surprise being lured unexpectedly into a situation and be mobbed, lynched or mysteriously taken away to be never seen again, literally!

I often wonder what my father would have said or done had he survived to such a grand age as that to live to tell about the worst war on us today. It is no longer to remember Kruschev banging his shoe on the General Assembly table shouting his voice over a ruling made by them against or for him. Indeed, today the spirit dies looking on at their horror, the worst offence targeting little children.

Chapter 1 : Early Life

Our house in Tokyo where we lived upon arriving back from Russia was a Japanese style house, with a large garden with a big pond with fishes swimming in it. I had a cat and I loved my cat, but behaved like a pagan animal to the pet, for I had had no religious education at all until I went to Kenwood Academy, the Sacred Heart School I will speak of. For instance, as a young child, I threw my poor cat into the toilet. Another time, I threw my cat into the air, but couldn't catch her. This was considered very naughty. My Dad used to shout at me a lot for my naughty behavior. I had a lot of friends, many of them were Americans and I remember well, how they visited me in my garden to play with me. It was a time of food rationing in Tokyo, and there wasn't a lot of food. I used to eat the flowers in the garden when I got hungry. Nobody really noticed it. I arrived back from Russia a very fat baby, and in one of the photographs, I look fatter than my own very thin and lean father! In Russia there was plenty of milk, for instance to nurture a young child that I was, and there was enough food and drink, so unlike Japan, at the same time. I became a skinny little girl eventually and have never really been beset by a health problem related to over-weight and kilos problems!

It was my own Mother's second marriage, to my father. She had been widowed, her husband who was much older, had died. He was in the military from a famous military family. Her great friends were the Asos, Mr Aso, being a prominent man in politics as well as in all social things, greatly known by upper class Japanese society. He was I believe a business acquaintance of my Mother. They were not necessarily very happy for her to re-marry my father, after his period in France, for he said and did too much to offend the Japanese Government by his very modern and western approach to life in Japan. He criticized Japan's antiquated feudal system, for instance, wishing to put Japan into a time fit for Napoleon Bonaparte's revolution. This did not go down well in Tokyo. However, he fell greatly in love with her and she was considered a beauty of her days, and was extremely eligible. They got married. They had me, eventually. I was born a baby in war-time.

As mentioned before, it takes a lot to handle any Revolution. We can call it love if you like or even passion. I think for me it is Napoleon Bonaparte's Revolutionary call which inspired Beethoven's music. This revolution was the stuff of romance. Romance hasn't ever lost it's touch completely, though it is not considered revolutionary anymore. I don't know if it is even popular these days, for the greater authority of the authoritarian types seem to take over and consume time money and waste for anybody to have the time to reflect that romance would employ less harsher and sharper ways of dealing with people, time and money. When they refer to romance they generally mean sex and even hard core. Often it is even organized! The horrors go on. This is not what everyone seeks in life and though it is an age of greater individual freedom, I doubt anything can beat a touch of the heart and romance at it's best. ! It's better for the health, and probably too for the wealth! Far be it for me or anyone to put the whole world into a huge drug war. This would clearly be a man or woman without a conscious with quite the evil eye cast on their fate. In another words, it is wrong to run people down, be it on the motorway, or in some other program for

Me with Johnny at summer camp in the early 1950s

Chapter 2 :
About Johnny and Peggy

When I first arrived in Manhattan, in about 1950, I stayed with the Murphys. He was a GI serving in Tokyo, under the Occupation of General McCarthy and my father found him through the Catholic Bishop of Tokyo. He was persuaded and agreed to send me to their home in New York City, where they would find a school for me to go as a day student. I was to stay with them in their Manhattan apartment where his children Peggy and Johnny lived together with his wife. I was awed by the arrival in New York, where many press photographers were waiting for me, and I was carried off the plane. I was then aged six years. They were Jews. They sent me to a school downtown, where I picked up bad language and swear words. I was not learning anything at all. One day Mrs Sawada arrived to pay a visit to us at the Murphys and got all the information about me and my school. She worked for the Bishop of Tokyo. She also saw me and spoke to me in Japanese, which was the first time, I had a chance at all since my arrival to understand what was going on and speak a language I could understand, at that age. She wrote a letter to my father insisting that I be taken away from the public school they were sending me to, and suggested I attend a Sacred Heart Boarding School in upper New York State. My father was shocked to hear her report, and immediately drew up plans to change it, and soon I was in Kenwood Academy or the Sacred Heart School in Albany, New York. I was put into uniforms, one dark blue for the day, and another pale grey for the night, or the evening. I learned to correct the bad language I had learned at the first school, and was chided well enough for using swears words. I was told with kindness not to slap people on the face, but just tell them for instance, "don't do that, I don't like it. " Eventually, I began to read and write and speak English very well, and found myself engaged with a lot of school friends who got along with each other. We found strong friendships at that early age, and I soon forgot New York City, and swear words, and bad manners were replaced by the manners and language of a finer young lady. I was six years old when I entered the Convent school. When term time ended in June, I had nowhere to go for my summer vacation, so I hads to stay behind for some of the summer. However, if my memory serves me well, I think I may have spent some of that first year holidaying with the Murphys and Johnny was my constant companion. I still have a faded photo of this time, and I appreciated going to summer camp to learn how to be a girl guide and learn to swim. I returned to school in the autumn, having had a fun holiday, after all, probably having spent my camp time somewhere in the Catskills. The second year, I became a convert to the Catholic religion, as I was born and brought up a Buddhist. My father gave his consent about this, and wrote letters to the good nuns, wishing to hear my progress in religious education. I wondered what Christian name I should chose for my baptism, and confirmation, and I think that my father wanted me to chose the name Agnes, for she was the patron saint of Rome, who had died in valor defending her chastity against the Roman soldiers. She was also a girl from the patrician class of that society. My Christening took place and the god-parents chosen in name were the doorman and his wife, who lived at the gates of the school.

Later that year, I had my confirmation and the name Maria was the one I chose, which was inspired by a young girl who was murdered by a gardener for refusing him. She was a 19th or early 20th century saint. She was Italian.

My Convent school was considered amongst one of the finest in the East Coast. There was a sister college which many catholic young women went to after attending the junior school which finished at University level. I studied at Kenwood from the age of 7 to 13. I left in about 1958. The college for older girls was called Manhattanville. When my father was posted from Ottawa, Canada to the U.N. in New York City, to be the Japanese Representative of the Mission of Japan to the United Nations I decided to change schools and go to the French Lycee in Manhattan, on the upper East side. This was about 1960.

The first days were exciting enough, with girls and boys there in my class-room, which did make a huge difference to me. I thought for sure, in my dreams that I would end up falling in love with every single boy there, but that was to become nothing but a laughing matter! We did not attend school to fall in love! We even suffered spring fever and the laughing illness once, but it never made ever any of us fall in love with each other! I think my Dad made the right decision in allowing me to attend that school for that year, but for his news to me that he was offered new posts to go to, and that by June, he must return to Tokyo to meet the Foreign Office officials about the new task ahead of him at the new designation. He asked me and Marita which country we wanted him to choose. He was offered the Court of St James in London, Paris, France or New Delhi, India. It was quite the choice. For my father, the career diplomat, New Delhi, India was the toughest one and the most prestigious one from the point of view of diplomacy.

beautifully groomed and coiffed. There was evidently a point for all this relating to the morale of the country. The Americans in the 50s were the heroes of every nation, in particular amongst them their Allies of the World War. The Japanese however were not of the same league at the time as they had fought against the allies for a victory over the Far East. However, the intelligent Americans learned a lot about Japanese art and culture and returned home enamoured by the customs and traditions of Japan no longer looking on the Japanese as the enemy of the Americans . This I have witnessed amongst fellow American company many times. They are really very different to the Europeans who keep and remember their old enemies of war, never troubling themselves to find out anything other than past fears or dislike of a former enemy of a different time. This is brought up every year in England by way of the services and commemoration to their War dead of both World Wars. I feel it a terrible shame that intolerance can pave the way for more discontent amongst the nations serving their individual countries be it at the U.N. or somewhere else . The nations that struggle to survive, I'm sure would rather place a wish in a fountain than disappoint all wishing for a better tomorrow and hope for a life with certain rewards at the end. Misery and bad treatment by inconsiderate bullies will not rebuild such a hope much less a faith at all. From this point of view, a very desperate man or woman might consider the popular song as more useful to the spirit and soul for a better end.

I used to lunch with him at the U.N. building where there was a restaurant on the top floor. They offered simple meals and salads. My father was sober, and hardly ever touched a drop unless socially he was required to.

Naturally, when we met, I was still under-aged, and drank the good New York water.

He loved entertaining, and did this with great generosity and good taste. He took care of his guests well enough to make them feel happy and comfortable, but in the process often found no time himself to eat any of the fine dinners. This was in part due to the absence of his own wife, my Mother, at these functions, as they were separated. On his way home, however, his chauffeur Robert stopped by a very ordinary and very New York hot dog stand and bought a hot dog for him to eat. This was enough compensation for the moment for my Dad, who must have been hungry by then. He didn't go to bed on a completely empty stomach, due to the driver's attention to him. Little things like this makes a great deal of difference to anybody in life, and I know how much, my father appreciated it.

During my student young life, living in Westchester and commuting to the French Lycee in Manhattan, every day, one of my class-mates was Nicole Le Vienne. She was the daughter of a famous film producer called Jack Le Vienne. He had made a film about the Second World War and Winston Churchill. He was well known in the New York City circuit. He was divorced from his French Algerian wife, and he was responsible for the schooling of their only daughter, being the beautiful look alike of Brigitte Bardot but many many years younger. When the Italian Prince Vittorio Emmanuel came for a visit to Manhattan, his escort and the girl chosen for him to be by his side, was in fact Nicole. Later on, many years after New York, when I was doing a fashion modeling course at Lucy Clayton fashion modelling school, I met up with her out of the blue in Conduit Street in London. There used to be a Danish sandwich place there, so we went in and had lunch together. It was nice seeing her again after so many years. She hadn't changed very much. Then we both went off on our way, and again many years passed, when at a reception held by an American girl-friend of mine and her husband, I was suddenly introduced to Jack le Vienne! In astonishment I asked if he was the same Jack le Vienne who was the father of Nicole. Yes, he replied, but you know she died. I was surprised and taken aback by the sudden news, and asked him for more. He told me she had acquired meningitis and had died of it aged 25. I said how I remembered how generous he had been to her when we were students in New York, and that she was the best dressed girl in the school. He replied that it was worth it for she was worth it. We continued to speak a little while longer, and I gave my condolences to him then and there. I think he appreciated this and liked knowing me for I was once a friend of his daughter!

Chapter 4 :
Kenwood Academy – Early Days

My early days at Kenwood began aged 7. As little children, we had a play-room and each girl had their own corner where they could keep their dolls and teddies. It was a light airy room and sunny when the sun shone. There was a canary in a cage. It was called CHIPPIE for Chipper. In the evening, before going up to our dormitory, the nun would sit us around her while she read a chapter of a children's book like Winnie-the-Pooh. She used to tell me for instance, that I was a little like Piglet, whereas she would tell another child, they were like Rabbit and so on. We all identified ourselves with one of the characters in the book which helped us to pay attention to her. After reading to us, she took out a box of sweets or chocolates from her big cupboard she kept under lock and key. We all delighted to be offered candy before she put it away and locked up the cupboard. We ran after her with quick steps, skipping and tripping along the corridor leading to our junior dormitory. We then had to take baths, brush our teeth and go to bed, with a little blue light on in a corner of the dormitory in case we had to get up in the middle of the night. The nun had her own cubicle with a curtain around it. She was always up before us and woke us up at 6. 30 every morning. There was always a window left ajar over-night, though it could get cold. Winter with ice and snow, left us freezing in bed! Once up in the morning, we had to stay in a line holding our sponge bags and our towel. We had to prepare for Chapel and Mass at 7. 30. This was the beginning of

Vermont

Back in New York, in about 1953, I was noticed by an older girl called Jeanette. She was one of the senior girls, while I was still in the junior school. She invited me to stay in her house in New England, and got permission from the head mistress to take me with her to meet her parents and stay the holiday with them. Her parents came to fetch us at school, and we were driven a long way until we reached Burlington Vermont. It was a house in town with a den and a large fireplace where we congregated and watched television. I was then about 8 years. Her mother couldn't have been a more caring or considerate woman who took an immediate love to me which I felt and trusted. She looked after me with kid gloves. I was very shy, and didn't dare talk and stayed in my room a lot, too shy to come out. It took time and patience to make me re-gain back my self-confidence enough to talk to them as any child has a right to. Eventually, this spell was broken and I never stopped talking to them after a week or more of silence due to that shyness. Even now, I am cautious when meeting people, and also very reserved a lot of the time in what I say in public. I even force myself to put on an act rather than speak openly or even genuinely to "strangers."

After our first meeting, the invitation was ever-lasting while the Mother and Father stayed alive, I was always welcomed there. After the death of Aunt Mary, I never really returned to Vermont to visit them anymore, for the children of Aunt Mary and Uncle Arthur can be difficult for me to explain without being a little mis-understood. All I know is that it is just as well that I keep my distance. The brother David is a materialistic man for his sister Jeanette who probably would stop at nothing to gain favors and greater wealth and power for her. She is an older lady in her mid seventies. I mind my head when he is around. It's best to protect it with my nuclear mushroom hat! A reason the bomb is on the agenda in the world of fashion as well. They talk so much about it. He had tried to win a seat once in politics as a democratic representative of that state. They say "never get involved with politics or politicians! " I think this is a fair summary of that position. As a result of the conflict, I have not returned to Vermont, to their state of the green mountain boys for many years, even avoiding going to pay my last respects at Aunt Mary's grave where she may rest in peace. That is a terrible shame.

At school, I had to go through all the studies offered by the best American style system of education. It was a case of do or die! No matter how poor my grades had been in geometry or in physics I had to study them regardless and get through them! Therefore my educational standard wasn't too bad though hardly excellent. We also had to do sports regardless of whether we were good in them or not. I played hockey and even got myself into the team playing other schools as a left wing, because I was a fast runner. This is essential for a wing. I played some basketball as well as ice skating and skiing during the season of winter sports on the slopes of Stowe Vermont, a famous resort where the Von Trappe family of Sound of Music fame rebuilt their lives after their escape from Nazi-occupied Austria. They used to sing choruses and often gave concerts in the summer time in the mountains and hills of their new home in Stowe. The Kennedy's, especially Jackie used to frequent this area for her winter sports. However, beware, for it is freezing there a lot of the time, and the snow drifts make it almost impossible to see one's way down the slopes. One learns to be tough when faced with extreme conditions like this. Life is not made for a softie! Apart from these activities, I learned to play the piano, and later on took lessons in the theory of music. I played many different piano pieces, and my teacher a Miss Knight had the tendency to get me to play Russian piano pieces rather than Mozart or Beethoven, though I did learn both on the piano. The only trouble with Russian classics is the reach of the hand is for a large hand rather than a small hand, and the exercise of playing was difficult and never fulfilling as I do not have a far reaching hand as they are smaller! She knew I wanted to play some Chopin but the only piece she allowed me to play when I first started taking lessons was the Prelude in A major, op 28 No. 7 and Beethoven's Ecossaise. Joanne Hearst, who was a much older girl, was the pianist and star of the show. She used to play piano concertos on two pianos with Miss Knight at the end of each year, and she had those hands which had a wide span. She was brilliant in her studies and over one summer holiday spent in Havana, Cuba, returned speaking fluent Spanish, for instance. She too took riding lessons, and looked crest-fallen when I received first prize for show jumping aged eleven or twelve years, but she had the courtesy to congratulate me, which was a trait going the right way for her. After all one must retain the better attitude of good sportsmanship in sports, even if one prefers not to remember manners in it sometimes.

We were together too in acting and drama as well as singing. I had a very good ear and always knew the note the singing started on, so I was put up there with the rest of the chorus and started the singing myself with that note. The drama was automatically a study for everyone in my class and we learned something by it. This again came naturally to me, and I found it very easy.

Once a week we were allowed to see the movie the school hired from outside. One of the movies was called "The Robe" with Richard Burton and Jean Simmons. Another was a film called "Lost Horizon" with Ronald Coleman and we even managed to see that Hollywood romantic story called "An Affair to Remember" and Audrey Hepburn in "Green Mansions" and "War and Peace". Later on, when I changed schools, I used to go to see movies with a boyfriend like " La Dolce Vita" and "Never on a Sunday" and the life story of the famous Italian artist with Gerard Philippe called "Modigliani". I was made the President of my class for two years, and this was nothing very difficult, except to have talks with my form in my school, and keep the class in order.

Chapter 5 :
Glen Cove, Long Island

When my father first arrived in New York, he looked for a house to rent, and found a beautiful old house in Glen Cove, Long Island. It is in Oyster Bay, and within commuting distance to Manhattan. It had its own private pier and we could go swimming in the summer time, in the Ocean. The house was like a small Prince's castle, where time was eternal and the peace of the woodland around offered a haven of beauty and rest. He had servants who had two young children, both boys. The rooms had wooden walls and large fire-places, and comfortable big sofas that one could sink into, even hide in the day or night, never to be discovered! I loved this house, and when the owner decided to put it up for sale, she offered the house to my father for quite a large sum of money, which my father did not have! I wanted him to buy it, and though he could have purchased it, I think the Government didn't want to buy it. He himself thought better of buying it privately. We then moved on to Westchester, and in the meanwhile, the famous Broadway production of "My Fair Lady" arrived with Julie Andrews and Rex Harrison, both English stars. Rex Harrison and his wife Kay Kendall, moved into the house after us, renting it. They were stars and they threw a lot of noisy parties and stayed on until the term of the Broadway musical had more or less come to an end, which was a long time. My father, when he did retire from the Foreign Office, bought a villa in Cap d'Antibes, South of France, called Le Theleirie, and he stayed there six months a year. He purchased this villa from a Belgian couple who had named it Le Theleirie, which was their horse that had won a famous horse race.

Like a kindred spirit following us, Rex Harrison also purchased a house in the South of France, in St Jean, Cap Ferrat. He did journalistic work and contributed to the community from England. At the time, there were quite famous stars from England, who had villas there as well, and certainly, Monte Carlo had many English residents, at that time. Now it is a new crowd of jet-setters, many from Russia and gangsters and drug barons from all over the world, who can afford the costly way of life there. Understandably it has become a racy life with threats and violence escalating into the realms of the ghetto but certainly the houses and the life if affordable can satisfy the most demanding customer. It is a new feel of life, and can be caught in extremely dangerous circumstances as explained. One sometimes has to have eyes behind one's head!

Rex Harrison's wife Kay Kendall had died while they were in the United States, and he never re-married. He would have known something about my famous Dad, as my father would surely have recognized his name. "By Jove, what a coincidence, " is probably what he would have said to my father, had they ever met at a party! This never came to pass. Even though they had never met, they were like old friends. I am certain of this.

Life in the City

Iknew many children of different Ambassadors in New York. One of my first boyfriends was the Italian Ambassador's son, who was studying law at Rome University, and who prided himself in having to take transatlantic flights several times a year to be with his parents and family for his vacations. We went out a lot, and saw movies, together. My new boyfriend, taught me a little of his law studies, and taught me too how spaghetti and pasta became the national meal of Italy from China. One of my other beaus was a French boy who drove a red sports convertible, who took me out to dinner once. He treated me to "frogs legs" which I tasted with some fear. It was nicer than I thought it would be, and reminded me a little of chicken meat. My girlfriend Barbara was the Swiss Ambassador's daughter. She was older by a year, and spoke four languages including English. She used to love the beatniks and the readings of Jean Paul Sartre! She was allowed to visit Greenwich Village in the day-time after school with friends, and it was the days of dives hidden in the street where black espresso coffee was served, and avant garde, rather strange eerie music was played. She thought it was all very "cool". Then there were the two Finnish boys, who lived in the same town as me in Westchester County, who I used to travel back with on the train from Grand Central Station. They were sweet. I think too, in hindsight, they were sweet on me! One Thomas lived in New York in America and the other Marc, lived with his divorced Mother in Lausanne, Switzerland, and helped her as she ran a very deluxe pension de famille. I myself was sent there for two summers aged thirteen, fourteen and a little of fifteen.

Growing up

One summer, which may have been that last summer, I wore a blue and white candy striped sun dress, which he loved. He told me he wanted me to marry him. I'm convinced it was the dress that prompted him to say this out of the blue. I was just going on 15, and he was about 17 or 18, just starting University, and I knew I had not the right to answer such a question as I was under-aged. We made no promises to each other, but I knew at that moment, we might one day decide to marry. However, after that summer, I actually never heard from him again, or saw him again. Childhood goes quickly like a dream, and what we think, do and say are fleeting moments of youth and their time, which we may remember or we may not do. I often wonder now about him or if he is even alive? Though a few old friends have resurfaced like ghosts from another era, when we were all of us "golden children" time hasn't taken away what we had as children or young adults. One never attempts to assassinate my friends because they know me and knew me as their friend , The slap on the cheek the Prime Minister received from one of his colleagues must be proof of trouble ahead!

Becoming of Age

In the meanwhile, Marita was staying at home with us in Bronxville more and more frequently. She told my father that I needed clothes, and asked him to pay for me to buy them, She accompanied me to all the shops. I had a nice wardrobe at the end. She returned to Santiago, Chile, and asked her own tailor to create some coats and evening dresses for me . They were a great success. I remember in those days, that French was the spoken language of diplomacy, so we dressed in a certain way according to that taste and as etiquette and protocol required. The dresses were always accompanied with their accessories. One must be dressed and adorned and must look as nice as possible, as a show of respect to the company one is with. These days, most people out in the street would not understand me as they dress designer but the look is to look as unsmart and as casual as possible. Very often, these are the signs of the times, and often one finds these people hard working, wealthy and gifted to a standard par excellence. They would never be without money no matter what they may not be qualified for.

After my year at the Lycee, I left having won a prize called the Prix de President or the Prize of the President of the school. This was an illustrated book of stained glass windows in the Cathedrals of France. Naturally, when I married and put my books on the book-shelf, I lost that book very mysteriously, as I also lost an illustrated book of Indian miniatures given to me by a friend from Jaipur, and yet another illustrated book by Aubrey Beardsley called "Salome" by Oscar Wilde given to me by George, an old

She was thrilled and all of us were very happy that evening. My father had to make plans and inform the Foreign Office about the future wedding and future Japanese Ambassadress in New Delhi, India. He himself had to leave for Tokyo in June, I was to stay with Peggy de Gripenberg in her Dakota Buildings apartment and continue my term until the end of June, and then he asked his fiancée what her plans would be. She replied she had much to arrange her life again before taking on a new life with us in India, and that she would be leaving any day now to return to Pretoria, South Africa to visit her Mother. She asked him if her Mother could live with us at the Embassy in India. My father made the mistake of agreeing to let her stay and live with us! I was to continue on to Lausanne Switzerland to stay at the pension de famille, and see her son again, before meeting up with my Dad in Geneva, where we would board a plane that would take us to Rome, and from there on to Beirut, Lebanon, and finally New Delhi, India, by August 1961.

India

India was hot, with a lot of new people for my Dad to meet. Marita had already arrived and was staying with Jose's cousin Miguel at the Chilean Embassy. The wedding was small but expensive. Marita wore a beautiful champagne coloured thick lace dress and jacket, and this is about all I can remember. I think her Mother was present, and my father was busy before and after so I hardly saw him to speak to him at all. There were many photographers and press from Japan and India taking a lot of official photos. They went on a honeymoon somewhere I can't remember anymore.

I will now list the Agreement made between the Governments of Japan and India, which enlightens the reader as to his reason for being in India in the first place.

AGREEMENT BETWEEN THE GOVERNMENT OF INDIA AND THE GOVERNMENT OF JAPAN FOR THE ESTABLISHMENT OF A TRAINING CENTRE FOR MARINE PRODUCTS PROCESSING

New Delhi, 31 March 1962.

The Government of Japan and the Government of India.

Earnestly desiring to advance the economic and technical cooperation between the two countries and thereby to strengthen further the friendly relations which traditionally exist between the two countries.

Article 1

There shall be established a Marine Processing training Centre(hereinafter called "The Centre" at Mangalore,

Mysore, India, the function of which shall be to render practical and theoretical training to technicians in marine products processing.

Article 11

In accordance with laws and regulations in force in Japan, the Government of Japan will take necessary measures to provide at their own expense the services of Japanese co-director and of requisite Japanese teaching and technical staff (herein after jointly called the "Japanese staff) as listed in Annex 1. 2.

The Japanese staff shall be granted privileged exemptions and benefits as admissible to experts assigned to India under the Colombo Plan.

Articles 111

In accordance with laws and regulations in force in Japan, the Government of Japan will take necessary measures to provide their own expense searching aids, machinery, equipment, tools and spare parts required for the establishment and operation of the centre as listed in Annex 11.

2. The articles referred to above shall become the property of the Government of India, upon being delivered c. i. f. at. The ports of Madras, Cochin, or Mangalore to the Indian authorities concerned.

3. These articles shall be utilized exclusively for the purpose of the Centre under the guidance of the Japanese co-director.

Article 1V

The Government of India undertake to bear claims, if any arise against the Japanese staff resulting from, occurring in the course of, or otherwise connected with the bona fide discharge of their functions in India covered by this Agreement.

Article V

The Government of India undertake to provide at their own expense:

a) an Indian director and requisite Indian technical and administrative staff as listed in Annex 111.

b) requisite building as listed in Annex 1V as well as land and incidental facilities required therefore.

c) facilities for landing marine products:

d)raw materials, replacements of machinery, equipment and tools, and any other materials necessary for the operation of the Centre and available in India:

2. The Government of India undertake to meet:

a) customs duties, internal taxes and other similar charges, if any, imposed in India in respect of the articles, referred to in Article 111:

b) expenses necessary for the transportation of the articles referred to in Article 111 within India as well as for the installation, operation and maintenance thereof:

c) any other running expenses necessary for the operation of the Centre.

The Government of India assume responsibility for providing , on payment of rent, adequate unfurnished housing accommodation for the Japanese staff and all pay Rs. 15 per day for each of the Japanese staff to enable them to meet the rent of the accommodation and the cost of furnishing their accommodation according to their requirements.

Article V1

The Japanese co-director shall be responsible for the technical matters pertaining to the functioning of the Centre referred to in Article 1, while the Indian director shall be entirely responsible for the administrative matters, of the Centre. There shall be close cooperation between the

remember their names. I think one was a relative of Nehru. At the time Nehru was the President. He invited many young people to a dinner held outdoors, once, and asked us a lot of questions about our impressions of India. I sat at the same table as him. One of my first Indian boyfriends was a Prince of Jaipur, whose famous step-mother, was once considered one of the most beautiful women in the world. It was to become a love affair too for him apparently, but this is only a rumor and mustn't be counted on as fact. They were, it is true not too far away from each other age-wise. However, I doubt even now the authenticity of the rumor that was circulating around him! After all, I was going out with him. I told Mr. Nehru that my father had allowed me to see the Taj Mahal in Agra, and gave him a fine reaction to the beautiful monument of the Prince who had created this mausoleum for the love of his wife. Later on, I remember Richard Burton saying that he wanted to give his wife, then Liz Taylor, the Taj Mahal, and found something else in it's place, as the Taj Mahal was not for sale. Otherwise, I lived an enclosed life in the compound, studying hard for my O LEVEL exams preparing myself for the English standard of education so alien to those that I already knew. It still remains a mystery to` this day, why Marita and my father sent me to Oxford to pass my A level, when all I wanted to do was return to New York to pass exams for University! My step-mother had other ideas and I'm not very sure at this time if they were good ones. She had never had children of her own up to then. The British High Commissioner and his wife recommended Beechlawn Tutorial College for me, and helped my father and Marita make this decision which must have completely changed my life. All I do know is that many people in the hierarchy here in England knew about my father and myself, and I don't think it was a pretty picture, which I agree I have paid penalties for in abundance. However, my father liked the life in England and forced me to stay on. This was followed by the children who also forced me to stay on.

Chapter 8 : Escapade

Our good Indian chauffeur Gokul had a great escape from the burning Cadillac being the official car of the Japanese Embassy when he drove my parents and two French friends staying with them from New York City, to a location outside Delhi, for a party and festivities with friends. Rosemarie always wore Christian Dior evening dresses and gowns, and all her clothes came from that house. The car set on fire suddenly as nobody had any wish, during that trip to watch Rosemarie's suitcase with the Dior clothes go up in flames. Gokul the driver valiantly got hold of the suitcases and saved the day not only for her but for the rest of the passengers and saved the clothes. What an adventure that nobody would forget easily. They managed to get themselves to the next small town, where help could be found and with another car hired for the rest of the journey, they arrived very late, but overjoyed at arriving at their destination with all their luggage. They all sat down and had a very good glass of well deserved Scotch! They toasted Gokul's who had saved the Christian Dior dresses from flames! After this, my father decided to buy a Rolls Royce, and came to London to chose a model and buy this out of his own pocket. He eventually chose a silver Phantom, and this was sent back to India, by ship. He lost the Rolls Royce lady on the front of the car, but they managed to find it, and he and Marita were as proud as two peacocks being driven around Delhi and India in this classic and proud English car. I myself had a drive in it a few times, but it was exclusively used by my father and Marita and guests only. Never again, they thought, would there be another incident like the burning Cadillac, and suitcases laden with jewels and expensive Dior gowns about to go up in flames again. This time, they could travel India in greater comfort and ease, and after my father's departure, the car was sold to the Indian Vice Chancellor.

on with them well. However the decision lay with the parents who were in New Delhi, far away from Europe! What a shame, the whole thing was. I never made it. I'm sorry it turned out that way. Notre Dame Cathedral was just in our view.

It was a matter of a few months after this meeting in Paris, that I saw RoseMarie and Bernard in Geneva. When I told her the news, she thought on it for a whole day. In the evening, she came down looking a little tired, and sat down in the study, where we usually gathered for our cocktail of the evening, which was a whisky sour, made with Johnny Walker Black Label. She suddenly said that she couldn't see why I shouldn't marry Leopoldo. As a matter of fact, it was the best news she had heard from me. After this, she reflected, and by the end of a couple of days, when we returned as usual to drink our cocktail, she said that she feared my age would not be an advantage. For this reason, and this reason alone, she didn't think I should marry Leopoldo. I myself was confused by then, and didn't know what in heavens name to think. She was influential. My father was not against the marriage, and in fact encouraged it. I met Leopoldo in Geneva after the two years, and decided it best to give up the whole idea of marrying him. I'm not sure if RoseMarie didn't play a role in this decision. I'm sure it had quite a lot to do with it than I would have imagined. I was certainly glad to see him again, and if circumstances had been different, who knows, maybe, I would have gone ahead with it!

As for Rosemarie and Bernard, they saw Sandra's father and mother every season in Venice. But they eventually distanced themselves from me, possibly because I myself had my own busy life, or possibly because they suffered a certain amount of sensitive reaction from Leopoldo's family. However, whatever my problem was at the time, I had serious set-backs from the hierarchy and much of this was in part due to my age and to some extent, due to my Nationality. However, marrying the future Italian Ambassador would have dispelled much of it, so I think. However, I remember, after my first child was born, when I was aged 26, I walked up a hill in St Paul de Vence, with my little 2 year baby girl, and we met MARC Chagall, a very handsome man, who had tears in his eyes, and approached me, saying I was very young, and was I the sister of the baby? It can't help either, if I look years younger than I already am.

To what extent this may have damaged my perspective future remains a little obvious to myself at least. Although I married Christopher, he was not Leopoldo, but a country boy whose father was a poor farmer. They were a large Catholic family, and they lived in a nice house large enough for the eleven brothers and sisters. It was a completely off situation, but everyone wanted me, in fact insisted that I marry. So I married. He was a bit secretive and betrayed my trust, for before I knew it, I had step-children!

My father dis-liked Christopher so much at the end for failing me both financially and morally, that he did a disappearing act, and refused to come visit us anymore, on the grounds that he could not and would not meet or see Christopher. I only mention this as some rumours try circulating about some enquiry as to my father's lack of attention to me. He never actually deserted me! The divorce would have ruined my reputation and as far as he was concerned, the marriage was a failure and there was no point for him to finance it for a better life with a man who could not support me after five or six years . He dis-appeared, probably staying mostly in Japan with occasional visits to Europe where he kept an eye on me and my daughter. To put it literally, his disappointment was greatest of all. At this point, he allowed me to look after those children, without considering what could happen to my own. It was all very crazy, but what need is there to say this, when my incarcerations in the hospitals to prove mental madness had to be part of the process of eliminating me, my own and my former! They called my former "monsieur le crazy" during the first Gulf War.

The other started that war, by a repayment he needed money for to give to a Jewish business man who he used to work for. The amount was not enormous in today's terms, but significantly enough to allow the war to conveyance the villa and even pull part of it down, to pay for his new career helping the Government win the financial war for drugs. Margaret Thatcher was the Prime Minister. It was understood that "their boy" needed their help. A very elaborate show of the war was built up for him alone. I was shot with injection which laid me up in France for over three months, suffering from yellow fever. My French companion ended up in the military hospital in Paris! Saddam Hussein was an ally then and a good soldier, who blasted Israel once with a missile or rocket and I felt glad for a change! I am human too. My girl paid for my stay at one of the best hotels on the Croisette in Cannes for three months. They phoned her when the war started, and she and all her friends staying in the villa were recalled. Later on, never will I forget the state of the dis-used and badly damaged house, but also the state and the contents of the refrigerator! I almost passed out, due to the fact that I was not completely recovered, and the heat of the day did not help matters there at all. The shutters upstairs were open and banging away. Half a wall had collapsed. The roof had been leaking. So it goes on, when I had to personally deal with the repairs and it's costs from the insurance man, who didn't know how to describe the damage, other than a "coup de foudre. " What I did do for the children, makes me ask myself, "was it worth it? "

Holidays

In 1985, I escaped to Tokyo, Japan, my birthplace. I arrived sometime in late August and stayed at the Okura Hotel. Nobody at my father's office in Chiyoda knew where he was. The secretary hadn't heard from him for months. We had an office block which my Dad created and completed by 1975 or 76, he found good tenants to occupy this small building opposite the Finance Ministry in one of the best areas of town. When I lived in Japan in 1967-68, the building had not yet been created, It was a beautiful residential house then, which Daddy rented out to Vishnu of the Ghana Embassy, who being a bachelor threw a lot of parties, and I became a regular visitor, together with all the other friends I had made that year 1967-68.

Chapter 10 : Tokyo 1967-8

Long ago, when I was in Tokyo, my father gave me my own home situated in Meguro, which is a fine residential area of town. It was a large American style house, with views over Tokyo. I was introduced to many people and even people in the press corps as well as young diplomats, most of them very eligible bachelors. We used to party a lot and have social reunions almost nightly. We even went skiing in the mountains as a party and slept in the same room, which showed what most young people did together in those days. There was nothing indecent in this, as we lived a little like students, and knew better than mismanage a situation amongst just friends. They were the good old days really, and I suppose none of us could have guessed that by the time I left Tokyo, somebody who knew me and my house in Meguro, had stolen my father's very fine Russian oil. It depicted the profile of a hitchhiker or a voyager in the winter carrying a ruck sack. I can only guess that somebody I knew stole that painting.

Chapter 11 : London

I was married only in Britain, but not in Japan, which is not the way to marry anyone from Japan. The marriage certificate validity was accepted in Japan however, as my father registered it with the area where I lived. It was on paper but not in action or in principle. Therefore, the conclusion was that I could only obtain my divorce in Britain.

When Christopher and I got married, in 1969, he made us members of the International Food and Wine Society as it was then called, catered by Andre Simon of London. Once a month, they had a lunch or dinner invitation which we normally went to in order to learn about wines and what it went with food-wise. My then husband loved it for the sake of the delicious quality food and wine. Daddy offered us many opportunities to eat and drink well, until we got the hang of it. He took us on holidays abroad, and we did eat and drink very well as usual. It is mischief to say or think he was a mean man. He couldn't have been kinder to us or more generous. I can't say however that Christopher shared my point of view that he was a good man, just as I could no more share his view that I have wicked vision and my eyes are ugly! This is something else. If he could never concentrate on the good offer and gesture to him or to me and our daughter, it is obvious, we were forced to split up and go our separate ways. Ingratitude is a monster to live with, they say. Here I agree. Grandpa doted on our daughter and was the proudest and happiest grandfather imaginable. It quite gave him a new breath of life and changed him completely. I shall remember my father always for the good times he could afford to give us by his kindness and enormous generosity. We visited France on many occasions, including a tour of the Loire valley and it's castles. He even bought us a summer villa in the South of France, which we had kept all these years until just recently when we sold it. We bought the villa in about 1972 and sold it in 2005.

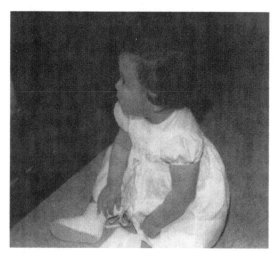

My daughter Helen Lisa Akiko, aged one year

In 1971, my Dad invited us for a holiday and sight-seeing in Japan. We left our baby daughter, then aged under one year, with the Norland nannies at the Norland Nursering Training College, which was then situated in Hungerford, Wiltshire. They have since then, moved to an area somewhere near Bath, in Taunton or Somerset.

We returned from Japan in early June, missing her first birthday by only a day or two. I remember phoning the nannies training college and being told how they were preparing her birthday cake for her. I was over-joyed to hear this news, missing my little baby girl, a lot, after a month's separation from her.

Now I will copy out a very old diary and record of this Japanese holiday with my father as "head guide! " It is written by my former husband who was prepared to release the diary to me, which I have decided not to copy out for the sake of wisdom and prudence. This was written for his firm which was the merchant bank he was then working for.

CHR
1st July 1971
A JAPANESE HOLIDAY

"My experience of Japan is limited to one visit for one month. It was a most exciting place because of the incredible activity and apparent wealth of the country, combined with the happiness of its people.

Tokyo was razed to the ground during the war, so now it consists of a massive commercial capital like any other big city, except that it is the largest in the world. There are many enormous departmental stores, where the choice of merchandise is unlimited. The Japanese love children and the children's department in these stores have to be seen to be believed. Goods in the shops are usually not expensive, but because the big departmental stores offer such a large choice they do include the most expensive items as well, e.g. they might contain an Yves Saint Laurent or Christian Dior boutique where a dress can cost up to several hundred pounds, or an exhibition of impressionist paintings costing hundreds of thousands of pounds.

In Tokyo we were entertained a great deal by the Mitsubishi Trust and Banking Corporation. The President, Mr Chikami , the Managing Director, Mr Tomoishi and several other employees took us out to a ten course lunch at a restaurant called "Kocho", which was in the basement of a building where Morgan Guaranty have their offices. It had a garden with plants grown by infra-red and ponds. You can relax in a Japanese restaurant because you have a room to yourself. Mr Tomoishi was so interested in Robert Fleming that he invited us again to the famous headquarters of all the Mitsubishi companies – Kaitokaku, which is designed for company employees to exchange courtesies and to receive guests. The Japanese companies are experts in entertaining – it is said that they spend more on entertaining than on dividends.

Before dinner we spent an hour discussing banking with members of Mitsubishi Trust's Foreign Department. Mitsubishi Trust is the nearest thing to a merchant bank Japan can provide. I had sixteen written questions to reply to on the City and its operations. In our honour the dinner consisted of a delicious French cuisine of the best class. It included smoked salmon and caviar and Chablis 1966, lobster, fillets of steak, asparagus, melon, strawberries, ice-cream, coffee and liqueurs. It was over by 9. 30 p. m.

In some of the best restaurants in Kyoto we ate beef with sugar and melons with salt – thus the flavours are brought out. We saw many temples – Sanzen, Hohzen, Jakkoin, Katsura, Nijo Castle, Shinjuan, Sanjugansendo, Daigo, Byodoin, Todaiji, Horyuyi and Toshodai – ji. Only photographs can describe their beauty, but in every case it depends upon their natural surroundings. All the Japanese school children visit them on school trips and thus they become the greatest travelers in the world.

After Kyoto we went to Ise, We saw the Daijinga shrine which is the simplest of all the shrines. Every 20 years the entire shrine is rebuilt and it takes 8 years to build. The cost

£4. 5million is raised from the faithful – thus they renew their faith! Apparently companies do not donate, it all comes from individuals.

We also went to Matsuzaka which is famous for its beef. This is the real farming district. The Japanese farmers are very rich and there is a surplus of 4 years rice stock piled. Land values are terrific and the billionaires in Japan are usually farmers who have sold out. Matsuzaka beef is massaged with beer and the cows are fed with beer. All the fat is dispersed evenly throughout the meat, thus there is no fat left on the edge.

We stayed one night near the Mikimoto pearl harbour. Mikimoto's motto was that he would strangle every woman's neck in the world with his pearls. He went broke two or three times because the plankton ate all his oysters. However, today it is a thriving business. We saw the pearl divers who dive into the freezing water to retrieve the oysters.

Once we stayed in a Japanese inn. Our quarters consisted of two rooms – the inner room had a large round table and tea with Japanese sweets were served as soon as we arrived. There was a sunken bath full of absolutely boiling water. We could not bath until we had walked about two hours for it to cool down. Our rooms looked onto a beautiful garden with ponds and lilies. The Japanese know how to relax and this they do easily. The people never seem to be overstrained and they seem to be able to pinch a few moments sleep anywhere.

We also stayed in a famous golf hotel "Kawana", which was full of Japanese business men, unaccompanied by their wives. They would get up at 6. 30a. m. to play golf. Everything the Japanese do they want to do perfectly. One has no idea of their enthusiasm, whether it is work or play.

In the evening there were films on gold. Golf as in France is only a top executive 's sport for the favoured few.

Because the Japanese look after you so well it is impossible to return other than with admiration and enthusiasm for them and their country. "

Medical record in London from 1971...

I will now tell my historical past here about the mental hospitals and what did occur in them for some years to come. In those days, they used electric shock treatments on the head as a way of calming down so called psychiatric phenomena. I was given twenty of them the first time, and unfortunately for me it erased all my memory of history which I had learned not only at school, as well as the rest of my entire education! I was in a hospital providing Mother and Baby care. My baby was in the hospital with me for a while. But eventually, because of the many electric shock treatments administered to me on that first hospitalization for the six months to follow, I forgot my baby and wasn't aware for a long time that she had been taken away and put into care somewhere else. After a few years this treatment was no longer recommended and taken off as a course of treatment. Due to a problem about financial health and wealth, the betterment for the doctor is often cited as a potential threat and problem sometimes. This obviously could be viewed too as a wonder drug for the stock exchange, The Royal Exchange here is cited being a potential bargain point for an investor? How much a "black out" is worth remains to be seen for a future in terms of money. Obviously there is no further use in any treatment if one should be so unlucky and be beheaded! This too or the guillotine in Paris, is now the unfortunate recommendation by the protesters going on against their criminals. Let us only hope we can better protect ourselves than fall victims and blame for the criminals! Only time can tell, and no doubt, that "bargaining point" is the secret that nobody tells about so far. I realize as always how it affects me.

Chapter 12 : Separation

Later on, when Christopher and I separated, I bought an album of Tales from the Vienna Woods by Johann Strauss, which became a favourite. We listened to this a lot as well as Bach's Christmas Oratorio. The children got used to listening to music from an early age, and I think adapted their taste earlier rather than later. The Bliss's meaning Joanne and second husband Charlie came for Christmas one year. We had a lovely time.

About my divorce

I applied for a divorce in 1987, which was delayed from 1985, due to the Houses of Parliament to permit me to divorce. This was due to the division in the family between myself and my own husband and the husband of the other woman who we know as the Tai. To all intents and purposes, my own husband had deserted me about two years after we married. He had a nervous breakdown while working for Robert Fleming, the merchant city bank in London, and had need of a lot of time to recover. I was alone at home a lot of the time wondering when he would return, which he did not do for many years.

In the meanwhile, I remember how the former Governor General of Canada and his wife came to call to have a talk with me over tea or coffee. She told me that she wanted my father to make sure that I did not lose the house I was living in, which was in Holland Park, in London, and that the ground and garden it had would and must remain mine for the sake of my child, a little girl then, called

Helen. She gave her a children's book by Richard Scarry, which I read to her.

Separation

At Christmastime, a few months later, the former Joanne Agle her second husband Charlie came to have Christmas lunch with us, which I prepared. We sat in our dining room which had a bay fronted window overlooking a camellia tree, which had a ledge on the inside of the front bay window. Joanne found this dining room most charming, and suggested I put a little sick bay of small plants in pots around the bay window and call it my "sick bay". It overlooked the surrounding garden outside and the beautiful tree we looked onto from that room was either a magnolia or camellia tree. She adored my daughter and Charlie was tickled pink because she loved eating peanuts. They took us to the new top of the Post Office Tower, which had a rotating roof to it overlooking London where they had a restaurant. I remarked on how Charlie knew how to eat a l'anglaise , ordering a welsh rarebit after he had eaten his main courses. It was a delight to see them, and my daughter had a lot of fun! They probably came to "cheer us up" as Christopher's name was hardly ever mentioned by them. When asked "where is Christopher? " I generally replied either "he's in hospital recovering from a break-down" or "I don't know! "

After they left, I busied myself after Christmas gathering a few small potted plants and promptly put them on the bay window. It was young Helen's job to help me water them!

I once took myself out and went shopping for a new evening dress. I passed Valentino, Yves Saint Laurent, Joseph, and other shops. Eventually I went into one of the shops and tried on a red dress. I bought it without thinking

I looked particularly spectacular in it. I already had a long red evening dress by Dior, This was no big deal but when I wore it repeatedly, I must say I always received many compliments and praises on how lovely I looked, so different from the usual silence or reserve! As I said before, I had five children and only one it would appear has survived. The boy was attacked yesterday and I don't know if he survived. The father was not the same father as the father of the daughter from my marriage. It's obvious we are not born angels in the world although we try hard to improve ourselves. Now, we have no more secrets anymore with each other as we are under the domination of dealers who hold us back. It's sad when it is all over, and breaking up can be hard especially after so many years.

Flying lessons 1975

When my very young daughter started school and was away most of the day, I was encouraged by a neighbor who lived a few doors down from us in Holland Park, to take up flying lessons. She took me to Elstreet aerodrome, where I embarked on lessons to take my pilot's license. In order to take these lessons, I had to have a physical examination and eye-sight testing, and as I was passed through as fit and well, with good eye-sight, I was permitted to join the aerodrome and commence lessons for a pilots training course. It was not all that difficult but I hardly started the course, when my father heard of it, and in a rage for fear I would be involved in a crash, he immediately reduced my allowances so that I could no longer afford to continue them. At £80. 00 a lesson, which in those days was very expensive, and I speak now of the seventies, it was hardly an occupation taken up by people with small incomes! Since then, I haven't had any free time to consider taking this course again, and certainly one cannot take it without a car and a proper driving license. A few years ago, the psychiatrist who didn't like me having the driving licvence removed it by telling me to present my case to the DHL to explain that I had just left hospital. The doctor didn't know if I could drive my car or keep my license. This was neither necessary to do or very fair. It turned out the doctor in question was looking for a better income and at the end got entitled to £150, 000 per annum extra from my account when it was held by the Public trustee in Kingsway, London.

My Holidays 1974 -1980

Years ago, when my daughter was a little girl, I decided on the spur of the moment to take the first air-craft at Heathrow airport to fly me to the first destination in Europe, where I could get away from it all. I had a credit card, and ended up on my way to Barcelona, Spain. I stayed in a youth hostel, with no luggage and no over-night bag holding no toothbrush and toothpaste! I met a writer whose name I have forgotten, but we spent a night doing the town and looking in at bars and even cabarets to get a glimpse of night-life in Barcelona! The next day, he suggested I go by train to Sitges, a small resort by the sea, not far from Barcelona. I managed to get there, and didn't bother checking into the five star hotel, preferring to stay in a bed and breakfast for the night, owned by a Britisher. I spent the day looking around Sitges, and looked fondly at the various points of interest including things related to Henry the Navigator! I looked through his telescope and saw the blue sea beyond for miles and miles. It was a hot sunny day and I fell asleep on the beach, with no sun-tan lotion and managed to get my legs, arms and face completely burnt. In

vicinity. They had a large family, and they had connections with Sweden. I had arrived on a plane where there were two Frenchman on board the plane, and because they kept eyeing me, I eventually went up to them and started talking to them. They explained who they were and how they got together to come to America to visit California. They seemed to be nice enough boys and one of them turned out to be quite the formidable barrister in Paris, while the other had special influence in the world of cinema I believe. Their English was not so very good, but understandable. By the time we left the plane, we had become quite good friends. I was fetched by Bill, their hand at the ranch, who took me over San Francisco as he kept pointing out the lights at night over San Francisco. It was a long drive, possibly an hour, but when we arrived, it was so different from the South of France where I had just finished a two week break. The cold air and the crisp cleanliness of the country and woodland was a shock wave to my sensitive system. There I was shown a room which was next to the big house. It was larger and more comfortable. After dinner, I retired early and exhausted. The next morning or the morning after that, I met everybody who was staying as guests of the Wassermans, who were a set often, invited everywhere. She had been a good friend of another New York socialite called Mardi Hughes. Mrs. Wasserman before she married, had been a reporter in Paris during the war and spoke wrote and read French fluently. She was not particularly beautiful. Her husband Bill was a famous American businessman. He used to play the stock market on his sofa everyday by telephone. He always kept a mistress, being six foot tall and very handsome. His mistress was housed somewhere outside Manhattan, and they had been together for many years. I think when he died, in his Will, he had left something for her as well, and I know his wife Miriam knew all about it, but it never upset her status as his wife. They had children who had married, and they had many nieces, nephews and friends from abroad, which I was included to be amongst. It was Peggy de Gripenberg who got her to invite me. Peggy was the wife of the former Ambassador of both the United States and the United Nations. He was apparently a difficult man but having never met him, I can offer no comment, except to say that he was apparently extremely handsome. At one time, she lived in the United States working where she caught a good friend in my father, then working as the Japanese Ambassador to the United Nations, and then her husband was living back home in Finland. Their one daughter was married to a businessman in North Carolina, where I used to visit her, when she was still alive, though very, very old. At the time of my visit to Christmas tree ranch, I was considering divorcing Christopher Randag. Mrs. Wasserman didn't like this at all, and tried to persuade me to stay on being married. She asked me what sort of a family he came from, and who his brothers and sisters were and what sort of life they lived. To all intents and purposes she didn't quite understand the problem as usual, because I never told her. She and Peggy later on fell out with each other about the divorce, and to her grave she went, never truly understanding the nature of my problem with "Christopher. " However, she was prepared to invite the two Frenchman I had befriended called Jacques and Pascal. She served wild boar in their honour and was greatly charmed by them. She spoke French to them, and they were very pleased to meet someone who spoke their own language. It was an evening of some cordiality and friendliness the evening through. We engaged ourselves and planned a motor trip down the Big Sur through Carmel to Los Angeles together at an appointed date. I had Mr and Mrs Wasserman's approval about this.

We met many of her young friends, which was a household full of them. There was a French girl who was my age, whose father worked at Air France, who I befriended at the time. Her name was Vivianne She loved horses. One day, after a breakfast with a lot of young people both girls and boys around a huge kitchen table where the Austrian cook made lots of hotcakes for us to eat with maple syrup and crispy bacon, steaming coffee and milk, Bill marched us all out to the stables , and decided to take us all riding. I was put on a horse, and had to ride with the rest of them. I was grateful from my previous riding lessons, as Bill didn't know I could ride so well. Suddenly, he said, we're going to go for a canter now, so we all cantered, until he speeded up his pace and we were soon into a full gallop. Suddenly my horse veered and tried to throw me off. He had stepped on a snake, and was galloping wildly after this. I think I fell off. I had lost control of the horse, and I also felt a sting on my leg. After this, they eventually came back home. My legs suddenly got huge and uncomfortable with a burning sensation. By this time, I had gone into San Francisco, where I stayed in a motel near the house of Joanne's mother. Joanne gave a party for me where I met again a lot of young people. One of them, a Jimmy invited me to stay in a house which he was looking after for a family together with another friend of the family during the summer vacation. He said there was plenty of room and I could come and go as I liked, if I wanted to travel but have a base to come back to. By this time, I had hired a car, which was some sort of a Pinto sports car. I zoomed around in this car, and met up with two Swedish friends from Christmas Tree ranch, where we hoped to travel north to see the Cascades. In the middle of the journey, my legs from the horse bite, were so swollen, they were positively enormous and uncomfortable. I had to stop, and we stayed in an empty house belonging to some friends of a student jewellery designer who was traveling with me whose origin was Swedish but she lived in Michigan. The boy was related to her, and came from Sweden. When the couple returned that evening, he looked at my uncomfortable legs, and the next morning took me to the local hospital of Mendocino County. I was diagnosed as having suffered a bite of some sort resulting in my swollen legs, and advised not to ride horses again, as the birth of my baby had caused this out-break. He told me to put my legs up very high, as much as eight to ten pillows high which would help the swelling. He put me on a course of tablets, and after a few days, I was almost recovered. The traveling companions were awfully sweet to put up with my illness, but eventually we decided to return to San Francisco. I think they were meeting other friends there by a certain date, and we returned.

Jimmy and the other boy were a bit gay-ish. I met Bob a film actor through an Englishman called Terry. Terry told me he had boarded a grey hound bus one day on a tour of the United States from Britain and when he arrived in San Francisco one day, he fell in love with it and decided he had found the natural place for his home. He had a big apartment or house in Divisidero, and had a job. He went to clubs a lot and knew a lot of people in the acting world. His friend Bob lived in Carmel. We joined up with them with Jacques and Pascal at his house in Carmel on the way to Big Sur and Los Angeles. It was all very wild, and I didn't enjoy it all that much, because they were all a lot of men fooling around with other men from other groups about something I couldn't understand or care about. I went to bed and slept while they cavorted around Carmel.

After returning to San Francisco, I did a tour alone to Nevada where I made it to a gambling resort. Again the drive was interesting and I saw the famous Death Valley. I also passed Sioux Valley. I went gambling in the casino of the hotel, somewhere near Las Vegas, but didn't do well playing black jack, so I didn't stay at the table to play to lose! I was glad to be in bed for the long hot dusty road had made me tired. I almost fell asleep at the wheel of my car and had to pull the car over to have a rest for fear of having a car accident. I also continued on to Lake Tahoe where I went on a boat ride with a young man whose name I have forgotten after so many years, but we had a nice talk about whatever, and the surrounding mountains and the clarity of the water in the lake were unforgettable. I did not stay long. It was a stop-over. My legs were still not completely right, and some discomfort still existed. Upon my return, I decided my finances were hardly marvelous, so I said my goodbyes to a lot of people I had met that one month, including phoning my hosts at Christmas Tree Ranch, as well as Joanne and her mother to say thank you again and "what a lovely time I've had". The one month break had done me a lot of good, and I had made many more friends than I had expected. I returned to London. I missed my American breakfasts and hot American coffee. However I was glad to see my baby and didn't I make such a fuss over her. I was also appreciative of the good Norland nanny I had at the time looking over my baby. I was in fact very glad to see them both.

My solicitor, then a Mr. Jefferson, wrote me a line saying "Surf Up? " This was a new album by the Beach

Boys. We used to listen a lot to the Beach Boys those days, when I was so very much younger!

Chapter 13 : Reconciliation

Eventually a man who looked a lot like Christopher came back home to stay with us as it was apparent he had been away a long time. This is how I created a brilliant career for myself for many little girls like my own daughter, who accepted me as "Mummy" or as the French would interpret as maman or "ma mere" as addressing a good nun in a Sacred Heart Boarding school, like the one I attended in Albany, New York years before. He respectively was accepted as "daddy" or "mon pere" as one addresses a priest in a religious dominated school for boys or at a church! In the "Sound of Music" which we went to see with the children, there was a song about the nanny goat and billy goat as puppets in one of the scenes. Unexpectedly, Christopher claimed that he was "billy goat" and called me "nanny goat". We laughed a lot about it as though we almost knew how true this was in reality! We were bound by silence to accept the order to look after the Tai children who were not my own, for the sake of the separation that had developed between my own husband and myself. In fact, I lost the custody of my daughter, through an authority, be it French or English. It had to do with the head of the French Rail, whose popularity with the social workers in the social services, led them to betray my own children and let them down for the sake of protecting and being the substitute mother for them, whose own mothers cared not to see them or look after them. It was a case of their Taiwanese mother who tried to be "similar" to me, so that she could be mistaken for me to the extent that my own father would agree to leaving the family fortune for her instead of to me. Once when she met him, she tried asking him to leave money for herself and for her own children . My father was angered by her request and her selfishness and said positively no to her. It is odd how she spoke to someone and complained about his refusal to her. She organized it so that eventually she stunned my father with a shock that nearly killed him. It is stranger still that when my good father did die, all the inheritance money was organized to be given over to her and to her side of the family by the Official Solicitor and a man named Marco. I am always told how I spend my money unnecessarily these days taking taxis or mini cabs. I explain that it cannot bring me my fortune to take public transport. It is a stranger story still to tell when my Application to the Court of Protection is delayed without time, because two people have approached them with their Application to be allowed to do a bank robbery, possibly on my capital account! I have already asked an American Attorney in New York to take over as Deputy for my account and also to act for me in a civil case regarding a debt that is still owed to me by the Labour Government. I have heard rumours that the Officials want that debt money to be returned to an unworthy candidate, calling herself Helen MA who has a lien on the public transport system and was once Norman the wife of Mr Major. It is all a kinkie story and weird characters who play a part in a coup against me for that prize-the MONEY! The unpleasant experiences too tells me how they waste my time trying to prove I should be redundant sexually by the mis-understanding that I am too unfit to love or have boyfriends! This is very omnipotent and they decree it for their inhumane and cruel so that their reasons for finishing my love life(the doctor)proves how immoral they are and unruly to the point of unlawfulness.

For instance they are prepared to breach my security and peace as well as try destroying my health. They are even prepared to desecrate my body in a show of what they think my worth is as a woman. I agree the doctors should be thrown out! Much of the protests comes from homosexuals, lesbians and prostitutes who are the ones responsible for attempts to overthrow me as a woman. This constant need to overthrow me as a woman has often prevented me from seeing my family including the grandchildren, who in turn can be put at risk. The waste of time is the most marked instance one experiences through these manifestations of disorder be it mental or otherwise. Certain torture here is recognized and acknowledged and it is torture both physical and mental. It is governmental and not the feat of a lay person. There's no way one can afford to start drinking champagne like a film of years gone by, while waiting for the chance of a lifetime to leave war torn Europe to fly to the free United States not experiencing the terrible war that is about to explode somewhere in the world. The plans of this Government says it always had to be for Tony Blair and his wars.

A waste of time

There has been a social revolution where the only way to get to know or see your friends is by being a telephone operator or a poa. If this is prevented by the mental health act or by the government, then why does nobody change it for me I ask myself many times. Why am I excluded and prevented from progressing to keep up with the times? If I haven't anyone's telephone number or address then I cannot get in touch with them. If the Government do not allow me full vision to see the transparent and invisible which is possible to do, I feel I am being cheated about things which even my own cat is allowed into for the sake of being a privileged cat more so than the owner. I am most underprivileged put to task and chores like a slave girl. This has become by now a tenure of my stay and my existence for it. I do complain about it, mind you. I think it likely I will not be treated like this or in a similar vein abroad, should I be lucky enough to be able to make it. I am treated sometimes with harshness and prejudice by the present Receiver or Deputy who is Michael S T. I need a full "regime change" to go through without losing all my money for I need a lot of money to take on the case of the debt owed to me, with a detailed analysis and enquiry of my convictions for the court room if it amounts to that. All this is helped better if I had full capacity to vision and to the know. Here I think I am up against a potential blockade. However if I do not succeeed, at least I can still rely on my money to support myself with. It is counter-productive to win my Application for the American legal to replace my present British Receiver MST, and be told at the end of it that I've lost all my money. This has been what I understand to be MST's trouble offered to me from the beginning. I have often felt he drives to "run me down" and my economy being his target for a show of his scorn and personal grudge against a healthier economy say over his own. He may well be one of the British who wants my all and my wealth not necessarily for himself but for the two who try to push their Application through to allow them to commit a bank robbery! Michael knows both people who are socially acquainted with him shall we put it that way. This presently is the course set before us. One has noticed in the past conduct of my company in Tokyo, that the business side was a case for "the pay and something I now refer to as the Taipei syndrome" meaning just that. The

homosexuality and agree to being his wife again. It is to ask for nothing at all and to receive nothing at all. We are divorced. It is just to go over a lot of old history all over again. Without going into all of it, after I gave birth to my baby, he told me I should stop eating because I was fat. He wanted to help himself to all the food. He wanted me to look like a skinny boy. Eventually I suffered post natal depression and anorexia. At the hospital where I stayed for six months in a mother and baby unit, they put me on medicine to increase my appetite so that I started eating normally again. I was allowed a love affair with a young man who I still hear about and who I still stay "true" to. We had a child. It was a complete twin of my first child and an adorable little girl! My father actually took a broad view about this, and didn't seem to mind a bit. The new boyfriend didn't like CHR starving me and the two were adversaries or rivals of each other. CHR admits to being homosexual. He goes on and on even now about my refusing him a better sexual deal. We are of course divorced. I think sometimes he is prepared to take it to the world court. He regards my status as a woman not allowed to practice love affairs and live with another man. He hoped to be my lord and master etc. I am not sure who exactly is "disturbed"I'd say he should leave alone for I cannot love him.

I am "innocent" in the case history created by a jealous woman in circumstances surrounded by a certain intrigue to give evidence of my mental instability which was to be her big cover up for the eventual financial redemption she waited for during those years under a type of siege by a doctor and his bogus attempts to cover up this evidence. He justified it by saying he saw no bad in her, yet saw so much evil in me. There are some who believe in their railway mother and her children, and once we were friends(the children and me) but by now, our relationship has not survived the many tests put before us.

CHR can be a devil kidnapping my "ally" and putting them into chains for as much as a year, until their will and mind is bent enough to accept they can never be a friend to me again or see me for that matter except from a distance. He ends up convicting everyone this way. He practices a fair amount of torture and mental cruelty himself.

They call me "vrain" meaning I am the true and the vain. This is a continuation of the desecration of my body for my wear meaning my clothes. Their Jew wants to steal my clothes. I have not allowed myself to leave my house often because of the security problem. I do not have new clothes except a fur lined raincoat, which I bought for the sake of the constant double pneumonia I suffer each winter season due to my repressed TB. Naturally their whore-lee stole this coat substituting it for something ill fitting .

The Jew wants to find another "BOB" the second husband's name who married her but it did not survive a long term ending or resulting in divorce. She now wants my "beau". I think it is wrong to interfere or tamper with bonded people who have known each other for over fifty years, and I would have thought she can find somebody else. However I doubt he will marry. He isn't inclined to. I doubt he ever would agree to anything other than live with Julie. She is the one he cares for.

It was all apparently for the waste of time bearing in mind that possibly Christmastime will deliver a great war meaning a world war for nuclears. " God save us all". It is expensive to fight nuclear wars and genocide the enemy.

All this concludes that CHR does it all and agrees to it all to make me feel ashamed of myself. This I think in all honesty is terribly homosexual in belief thought and feeling! He often gets his wires crossed.

Now I will go back to the story related to my security and the lack of it for my kidnapped little daughter, aged about 4. They drew up exchanges so very early in my own daughter's life. If we could all be so lucky to have a saviour like their Chao, head of Francrail, to take control in such a fashion and with such ambitious claims for their Tai's future as well- wouldn't it be loverly? Better than selling flowers in the street! They lived in a fine welfare state as they grew up. Regardless we became much later on a united and happy family unit and tried our best to make the best of it. I hope we were successful . They grew up sweet kindly and intelligent folk, whose greatest mis-fortune was the death of their grand-father, my father, and the provision of my stay under a mental health act and Court of Protection Order, which tied me up in many ways, controlled manipulated and harassed for money and a lot more than this. It has been a torturous path with many in contortions if ever I get my way, which is practically never, at least these past years between 1993-2007! The loss of money for me has been annihilistic in more ways than one, and I know how drug taking amongst all has been the blame of the case and losses of money, which I suspect will probably take time to stop,

Their patient Christopher and I used to play Italian lute music a lot on our old record player, and otherwise enjoyed evenings at home, either entertaining or listening to music or reading books. We lived in a large Regency house, on five floors, with beautiful works of art given me by my doting father. It was resplendent and full of my father's idea of good taste as well as a certain grand design to all he gave us to beautify our home that to many, it was considered one of the finest homes in the area, which was worth considerably more within a period of a few years, reaching £1million when I had paid £90, 000 for it originally, five years previously! However, after the divorce, I never bought another permanent home for myself as there seemed to be some trouble about the money "grand-pa" had left us, myself a beneficiary of the Trust.

In the evenings, we often sat in the drawing room, reading books, and listening to renaissance lute music which I have listened to again of late. I remark how it drives me mad, and I know their Taiwanese mother always drove me mad! Sometimes we listened to Beethoven's Pastoral symphony, to remind us what we were together for. Christopher often listened to Alistair Cooke's letter from America on BBC radio on Sunday morning, and we always attended Sunday Mass, taking young Helen with us.

In our summer villa, in the South of France where we went every summer, we had to entertain the children, and set up a stage in the garden to do some comedy skits. They loved it and enjoyed the entertaining and comical Mummy and Daddy. She eventually gained momentum herself as a comedian on stage at school and was quite an impressive actress , later on. We had a small Yorkshire terrier, called Bonnie, who we cared for a lot, and she was a good friend for the child. At some stage of my younger years, I had acquired tuberculosis, without knowing it. It was only by 1985 on a trip to the U.S.A that I was given a full medical examination including a test for TB. The reader can imagine my surprise at my being told that the test was positive, and that I had suffered TB for sometime but due to my age, was unable to give it to other people! This is what the psychiatrist wanted for me, by the drug or

land-lords seemed to mind their own business and be not at all bothersome. I was quite a contented tenant. Helen came to stay for Christmas. She loved the small Japanese restaurant near my apartment, where they served only Japanese food. At the age of fifteen, she unashamedly drank sake! In those days, our children were allowed possibly more of a leeway and rope space for party time drinks. She had a sensible time of it, and made herself completely at home treating it just as if she was in London, except in Tokyo. Instead of going to Kensington Gardens, we would take a walk in Meiji Gardens for instance. If she wanted to buy something, instead of going to Peter Jones, we went to Takashimaya or Seibu. I found a Japanese language instructor for her. She picked up the language much faster than me and could handle the writing and calligraphy much better than me. It is a language easier to learn when young rather than when it is too late, obviously.

After Christmas, she returned to London just before New Year. She attended a party to celebrate New Year's in, which was a Ball she had been invited to. I know she was most excited about this Ball.

As, for me, I befriended and had a short affair with a younger man, who came from Canada. I met him at my Shinjuku Japanese language course. By the end of six months, he spoke, read and wrote Japanese reasonably fluently, though his accent was awful to say the least. I returned to London, to face the music with the doctors, and with the lawyers concerning a belief that I should seek a divorce from Christopher. This was around April 1985.

*Tim and a Japanese friend who worked in Tokyo as a Sony
dealer in Kamakura, spring 1985*

Divorce

Eventually I had to leave my family at home, and take a
flight to Japan, where I had decided to settle down, avoiding
their master plan to certify me for the doctor to do to me as
he willed, without any interference from anyone, for this
was the offer made by their Christopher, so he could realize
a lot of money for himself and his daughters, by getting me
quietly out of the way.

For all intents and purposes, we divorced. I filed for one
upon my return with the Canadian Tim, who I befriended
during my time in Tokyo. He recently died here in
London. He was aged about 40. Because the divorce was
against their Christopher rather than my own former

husband, who had literally deserted me, the financial settlement after the death of my own father in 1994, went to his family being the Tais or the Taiwanese. My own never attended the divorce Hearing or made any claims for or against me. This is how my side and my children lost out on a lot, had it not been for my father's solicitor, Michael, who I still know and do go and visit at his offices in the city. He may have saved the situation to an extent.

Some years ago, on a New York visit, I remember how a group of British youths seemed to have followed me into a coffee place for a sandwich, and how awfully rude they were to me speaking about me in a bad way. The waitress at the counter serving got upset and asked them "Why are you so awful to her? " They replied "We do it for our country. " She was speechless, and so was I. The Romans used to say in ancient Rome, "eat drink and be merry, for tomorrow we may die. " Another way of saying it is "you can't take it to the grave with you" not even such worthless memories like this.

"It's all for me"

By now, 2007, I realized the little Yorkies, Bonnie and Boseley were the "crime" for they were the ones welcomed to both the U.S.A and France, which made the impediment and the claim for the British, that it was all to be for them! Both dogs are deceased, and I do not intend to buy another as the former husband wishes I do. I have a fine black Siamese cat, who is independent and can look after himself better than any dog can do, and is also affectionate and intelligent with me. He is also very clean. I live contentedly with him though he is an adventurer and has returned twice with two little birds he has caught in his mouth, and a

butterfly as well as worms, a rat and a mouse. He is
definitely a hunting cat!

Chapter 14

I will now copy out a letter marked Confidential, written from a solicitor who worked at the Law Society.

CONFIDENTIAL

22 September 2001
From the Law Society

Dear Mrs Matsudaira,
Re Taylor Joynson & Garrett

The whole matter relates to the estate left by your late father who died on the 4th May 1994, and you believe the threats and ambitions relating thereto of your ex-husband with regard to the vast amount of money involved in the estate. The last Will was prepared by the above and executed you state in April 93. The executors are the above firm appointed in the Will. A Deed of variation was prepared by the firm and executed on the 8th December 1995, which is not relevant so far as the Office is concerned.

I also ascertained that unfortunately you are under an order of the Court of Protection because you have been alleged and certified as unfit to manage your own affairs. The Public Trust office you state were the Receivers, but recently Michael Tuck of this above firm was appointed in place of the Trust office because he handles all financial matters for the estate and therefore obviously for yourself and your daughter at your request and under the terms of the will and Receiveship order.

You still have a case worker who is Roger Stern of the Guardianship Office. You confirmed to me that Drs Roth and Pare were the psychiatrists who recommended that you be made the subject of the Court of Protection, and you think they have been persuaded to take this action by your ex-husband who you state will stop at nothing to obtain the whole estate. You also confirmed when I questioned you on the matter, that you had tried to revoke the Receivership Order by seeing Dr Darendondo in Gloucestershire and that in fact you have been diagnosed as...

The basis of your complaint is that you wish to remove the above as Trustees of the estate and to free yourself of the Court of Protection Order and to be able to take control of your own life and although you admit that your allowance is generous , you would like a flat of your own in London, instead of using the house which belongs to your daughter.

I did clarify and explain to you that the Office cannot possibly deal with your type of complaint and that the only avenue open to you, if that is at all possible in view of the medical opinions, would be to remove the Court of Protection Order, and replace the above as trustees of the estate, but of course this is entirely a legal matter and you would require legal advice. The Office has no power...indeed you feel terribly threatened by your ex-husband and again you must seek legal advice as to whether anything can be done to protect you.

I fully sympathise with how you see your situation, and trust that I have been able to be of assistance to you in clarifying the issues involved.

Yours sincerely,

It is difficult to discuss in this book without getting "political" their "political correctness" in a government which refuses to obey some rule about crime and their manifestations in a secret war and conspiracy to save the lives of their pornography and sleaze. I only mention here how their violence is normally most upsetting for families. Their cause however is trying to be a cause celebre. After all how old their rent boys for sex are, is not talked of at all. They employ them for money. Too much sex, drugs and money has made it a field akin to a graveyard where none will talk, and the vow of silence continues to haunt many. What a shame to lament about.

Education has been changed for a bringing up of children in a drug culture, rather than a more traditional way of educational standards, resulting in many violent deaths and related crimes in inner and urban life.

Divorce time after I was put into Receivership by the request of my former husband after my divorce in 1987. This application only went through in 1992. I will now give examples of holidays I took under the government Receivership and how I became a patient of their Court of Protection. The essence of my Receivership Order was actually financial related to the financial settlement in my divorce case, where I gained 99% of the proceeds of the same of the "matrimonial home. " Christopher did his best to apply himself in the divorce case, signaling to the Court room that I was too unwell to look after myself and had therefore no right to divorce him! This was considered irrelevant to the case in hand, and I won my divorce, gaining my Decrees both on the same day, with a certificate for each Decree dated on two different dates, at the same time and the same day of the final Hearing. The actual barrister was my present father-in-law of my daughter, who married one of his sons in 2000.

Letters

Dear Ms Matsudaira

I am writing in the hope that you may be able to help me with my query relating to your telephone bills.

This morning we received two phone bills in your name, both of which relate to 5 Cheyne Gardens. The two telephone numbers on the bill on the bill are ..... .

I would be grateful if you could advise me if there is a reason for you having two telephone numbers.

Thank you for your assistance in this matter.

Yours sincerely

Garret O'Brien
RECEIVERSHIP DIVISION

★ ★ ★

9th May 1997

Dear Miss Matsudaira,

I am enclosing a copy of an invoice from Messrs Gander & White in the sum of £987 for a household move. When I spoke to them they said that you requested that certain items be packed up by the men and left on site at the flat. So far as I remember, you did not seek prior approval from this office for this expenditure. In that basis I shall be glad if you will clarify why it was considered necessary to pack up these items and leave them on site.

I look forward to hearing from you.

Yours sincerely
Miss C. M. GREENAWAY
RECEIVERSHIP DIVISION

Here in both letters, I detect measures of disapproval like a bad school girl who does not do it the way the school government want it to be done. Their authoritarianism here is remarked.

18th July 1997

Dear Toki

Your Will

I am sorry for the delay in replying to your recent request for a copy of your manuscript notes relating to your draft Will but I had to obtain our file back from storage.

I now have paper and I enclose a copy of the manuscript draft that your wrote out on 9th January 1997.

With kind regards

Yours sincerely,

Michael Stanford Tuck signed
Michael

My only comment here is his usage of my name and address to forward on mail to another girl unrelated to me with attention drawn to her Will specifying her notes or her manuscript of her Will.

16thy April 1997

Dear Miss Matsudaira

Thank you for your letter of 8th April.

I have recently received an estimate from Jaguar Alarm Company for the installation of an entry phone system in the sum of £1296 & VAT.

The reason for this letter is because the estimate was obtained without prior approval from this office or without confirmation from your daughter that such alterations may be carried out to her property.

In future, I would be most obliged if you could discuss any proposed alterations to the property with your daughter before submitting your proposal for approval to this office. In any event, contractors should not be instructed without first seeking prior approval from this office please.

The installation of a new entry phone system would usually be the responsibility of the freeholders of the building. Can you please provide further details regarding the positioning of the System and whether the agents for the freeholders have given authorization , before I contact Jaguar Alarm System Company. With regard to the extra £450 per week allowance for the hotel accommodation, it is proposed that this allowance be cancelled with effect from Tuesday 15th April (unless I hear from you to the contrary) as the noisy builders are no longer working next door.
I look forward to hearing from you shortly.

Yours sincerely
AJ DUNN
RECEIVERSHIP DIVISION

I add these letters to show how I was treated by government civil servants in those days, due to the fact that I was considered unfit to look after myself and my money. One can understand my complaint about them!

30 April 1998

Dear Toki

I am pleased to announce that the Court of Protection has approved the arrangements for our meeting on 9th June 1998 at 2. 30p. m.

The Court is quite naturally anxious to keep the expense down and has agreed with my view that it would not be appropriate for the Official Solicitor to attend the meeting. He has no role whatsoever to play in your affairs, unless he is so directed by the Court. At the moment there is nothing for him to be involved with. In addition the Court of Protection is happy for Helen to attend but does not see any reason for John Rothwell to attend also.

This means that the meeting would be between the Master, the Receiver, you Helen and me.

Are there any particular items that you would like me to raise at the meeting? We will use the opportunity to have a general review of your financial affairs, now that the administration of your late father's estate is nearing completion. I expect the Master will also wish to review procedures for making sure that you have proper access to your funds, and keeping unnecessary expenses and this includes legal fees to a reasonable level.

I regard all of this as good progress and hope that you do as well.

With best wishes
MD STANFORD- TUCK

★ ★ ★

30 April 1998
Dear Toki

Your Will

I am pleased to say that the Court have decided that Dr Whitwell need not act as a witness to your Will, mainly because of the inconvenience of getting him to come from Bristol.

The witnesses would therefore be your GP and one of my senior solicitors here.

I would very much like to get this done before you go away and we agreed that the afternoon of Thursday 7th May would be the best time. This leaves only your GP on line up. Can you have a word with him and give me his number so that I may talk to him?

I hope you had a good time in Spain.

With best wishes.
Yours sincerely
Michael Stanford Tuck

Obviously the confusion is at it's peak here for I was told about the collision course for the worst the Will would take on if it was executed, besides which I never took a holiday in Spain which he has referred to.
Waterlane
Oakridge Lynch
Stroud Glos
22July 1997

Dear Mr Elmore,

Having tried unsuccessfully to contact you through Barclays Bank Chelsea, I write hoping this letter will eventually reach you.

There is a lot of chaos in London about Helen and her money. As you know about Helen's case, is there any chance we could consult you, as I realize you have retired, on a temporary basis as our own manager, or rather,

Helen's financial private manager at Barclays Bank? If you should entertain this idea, please let me know or please let John Rothwell know. He is on holiday until 30th July.

As for me, I am presently At the Priory Hospital, temporarily detained here in Bristol. I am still receiving a type of Gulf War Syndrome on account of smoking cigarettes.

Many of my family in London have deceased. I send this praying you can prevent further loss of lives and of course our money. We would be prepared to pay you privately or as our personal and financial manager. The receivership are hardly able to look after us is my dismal conclusion

With best regards
Yours truly.
Tokiko Randag Matsudaira

In this letter, I explain that after the financial divorce settlement in a case of marriage, as I was the only one married amongst that myriad of Chinese girls who gave unnecessary births to too many girls, my own x-husband and my own daughter out of wed-lock were never included in the financial observations required to pay them as the legitimate father or husband and daughter! This is the reason for my letter to Mr Elmore. Earlier, I have said that the psychiatrist killed the girl who had been looked after by my old Dutch school-friend and attacked him as well and I'm still not certain if Juste made it back to Holland alive or dead. The present situation viz a viz the psychiatrist and myself is perfectly clear. He intends to kill my own off-spring for the sake of her legitimacy and also wonder who is the one who is my own former husband from our wedding days! There is no doubt people are going around wearing facial masks to represent somebody else so that they are undetected. It's awful, and I'm sure everybody would agree. Very likely, though I shouldn't say it, this is the true conspiracy going on around me and the family which explains why we never meet or have any meaningful reunion. The walls have eyes!

Due to an incessant breach of security, due in part to psychiatric institutions, I have noted down that recently the United Nations sent me a body-guard. He was caught and taken by the medicals and psychiatrists, doped and I suppose he really did die. It is outrageous conduct and it disgusts me that the waste of time is so complete that there is no more use in taking their advice at all seriously for they are not always clear or truthful with me about their own reasons for the crimes. To clarify these points, I will now copy a few letters more to the various Court of protection managers I wrote a few years ago.

The Chief Executive
Public Guardianship office
Kingsway, WC2

Dear Sir,

Althought I wrote you a letter dated 13th June, I wanted to apologise for an error I made in the letter alleging that it was completely Michael Tuck's fault that I was a target for medical people. I doubt that this is necessarily completely true.

It has occurred to me that Roger Stone needs to explain himself. Although I have only spoken to him a few times since the change of the Receivership, one thing he said to me keeps coming back to me. He said over the telephone that I don't take enough medicine! This was during the time when the medical missiles were probably at their worst. I think he needs to explain himself and any reasons I have in thinking what I do presently of him. Was he trying to threaten me in some way? It was an abusive treatment which has reflected badly on the rest of my family, who were or are still being detained from what Mr Stone said to me over that telephone conversation. I think we are all fed up with that abusive treatment be it from doctors, psychiatrists or whoever. I had been told that my new case-worker is not Mr Stone but Michael Stanford-Tuck. Please let me know what authorization Mr Stone has over me or any in my family. This I do need to know. I would also like to know from you whether Miss Greenaway has any legal or civil rights over me or is considered an authority over me in anyway. I thought she had been removed from my case sometime ago. Please correct me if Iam wrong.

This is the extent of my letter to you today. I hope to hear from you with an explanation.

Yours sincerely
Mrs TR Matsudaira

This letter was eventually answered much later on when the axes fell on one and all when it came to paying for their pornography bill.

Miss Carolyn Greenaway was an habitué of heroin use for much longer than 25 years. She wanted her drug and this imposed certain sanctions over me, as she wanted my money to pay for her habit!

★ ★ ★

Office for the Supervision of Solicitors
Victoria Court
Leamington Spa. Warwickshire
13th June

Dear Sir

I write to complain about one of the solicitors at Taylor Joynson Garret of.......

My complaint is this: he is contacting many and various doctors and psychiatrists, most of them unknown to me who follow me wherever I go. He over-controls my spending for my flat. He retains the French cheque book at all times and now, he wants to use further restrictions and control over me and those involved in decorating my flat.

He breaches me security this way, and the medical missiles have been coming at me now for over one month. They are illegal. He is meant to be a lawyer. I see no sign of legality here. I am sometimes afraid for my life. Some people think it will not stop at this. It explains my complaint today.

Not long ago about a year before he died, when he looked after my own father, I know he allowed many doctors into my father's hotel bed-room and according to their treatment, he went into hospital a few times . He treats me medically for the financial affairs he looks after for me. ...I fear for the safety of my family and my little grand-son. I am not happy.... It's all; such a trial and done by fanatics who want money to buy drugs with.

He asked me at a meeting we had last month, if I was prepared to sell my Japanese company. I told him the Company would not be sold. The psychiatrists and doctors have no right to a power of attorney over our accounts, assets and properties..... .

Please let me know where my complaint will end up. He wanted to give away our inheritance money to the psychiatrists so I am told-a Chief Executive which I think unacceptable.

astonishment, I watched the horses start as usual, and in midcourse, they turned around and started running the other direction. The collision was catastrophic; that particular race had no real winner that day. The injured were taken to hospital, and the dead horses removed. It was all a very messy end! So much for my attempt to draw up a Will.

Office for the Supervision of Solicitors
Warwickshire
15 June 2001

PS There is some doubt about that medical bill which I think the solicitor has or knows about. I'm sure the case is less clear than I would make it out to be. So from my point of view, Michael Stanford-Tuck should give an explanation about my financial problems if it has become a legal or civil dispute amongst medical people, who may be threatening me or my family for the sake of trying to receive payments. It could be that some of the doctors are not threatening me. It seems very complicated.

Mrs TR Matsudaira

The only contact I have up to date presently is a man there called Roger Stone. This letter is self explanatory.

I was truly confused at one point as to who my new Receiver was. This confusion produced my letter of 13 June to yourselves. Please forgive my error and hope this case gets settled before too long. Apparently the Public Guardianship office still hold most of my money that they do not wish to give up. Some of them want some of the money to go to psychiatrists from the past who I have no ties with and who are no longer acting doctors. I think this is the essence of my difficulties with Roger Stone and Miss Greenaway.

Yours sincerely
Mrs TR Matsudaira

I suppose in a case of "libelle" that Miss Greenaway is asking me to give her , yet again, all my money, though she is no longer with the Court of Protection. She's telling me to pay all her outstanding costs and bills for the sake of her court of hookers. This is today's assessment of the case up to date, 12 August 2006.

From another point of view, these letters do reveal my waste of time trying to have any decent life in this country due to the high tolls and taxes they permit themselves to tax me with for obviously, in the Holy Land of Israel, one never pays enough for the Government agencies, their Social Security, Social Services, Police, international conspirators delaying it's progress by the new French crisis delivered in England by the assassination plots of any Suez crisis deal etc . I do not pay enough is their message to me. The home is a target for their invasion of gold diggers! WHAT A LIFE!

I will give an example now of a holiday situation when I was under their Court of Protection.

Recently, within the past seven years, I have visited the Bahamas and have enjoyed holidays in the Ocean Club in Paradise Island as well as Pink Sands Hotel, , in Harbour island. I once met Huntington Hartford, at a reception, in London, the creator of Ocean Club Hotel. I said as an opening line to him, who looked serious, "You sound like a state in the United States. " He replied: " Yes, I am in a state alright, and I have a terrible financial problem because I opened a hotel they don't like and said it was a bad idea to build . . They said I over-spent and so that's how I am in my state! " It was a conversation that went along those lines. Poor man, if he knew now how successful his enterprise has become, he would be the toast of any town today. Certainly the international jet set clamour to own a home in Nassau and Paradise Island and the Ocean Club is the most famous resort now in the whole world.

The owner was threatened by their Public Trustee's Office of London, who had followed me to Nassau who forced me to leave my bed in the middle of the night to police patrol the hotel area checking it all out in my pajamas and dressing gown. The next day, the owner of the hotels came past the swimming pool, and relaxed in the sun. Luckily, because of my police patrol, he survived. He had a retinue of people around him. His hotels are lots of fun to stay in and a must for any Caribbean holiday lover. Possibly the Pink Sands Hotel is the most famous one, as this is the one John Lennon used to visit when he was alive. At dusk, the sand turns pink.

Chapter 15

My religious instinct tells me to look at the lives of the saints. For instance I looked up Santa Lucia or Lucy in English. It says in the book the following: St. Lucy, Virgin of Syracuse who went with her mother to Cataminia in Sicily. Her mother is miraculously cured and gave all her money to charity. The pagan suitor Consul Pascashius denounced her as a Christian and she was ordered to be placed in a brothel but her four oxon who were to drag her there refused to move. To save herself for shame she plucked out her eyes (her attribute) and sent them to Pasachius on a plate. Another version is she was condemned to death in 304AD during the Diocletian persecution. Her teeth and eyes were pulled out. When she would not burn on a pyre she had her throat cut with a knife or dagger, another of her attributes. The lamp she carries may be a pun latin accusative of lux lucem – light - Lucia (Lucy). I have continued with a note after looking up the history of Santa Lucia. In it I have said that Dr Pare the self-proclaimed "eminent psychiatrist" reveals the case against him originating some 35 years ago when I had my eyes tested . I was given a full bill of health with 20\20 vision. The "eminent psychiatrist " lied to me when he told me I had poor vision with no real insight into my problems while he was talking to me straight in the face. The eye doctor told me I could fly a jet fighter – so good was my perfect vision – 1982? Since then, many years later, I read with glasses on, and being bi-focal, need another pair for viewing or driving a car etc. I have lost some vision which cancels my better and normal health by the intoxication of

Chapter 16 :
About an Important Social Worker

I remember as a young girl, when my father invited a social worker called Isabelle de France, who was working in New York at the time. This would have been around 1957 1958. She told my father that a social worker's job was hard, for they deal with people in need from troubled homes, often violent and unloving. For many reasons which I cannot now go into, she told my father over lunch, which was an Imperial duck dinner, considered a fine meal for a grand occasion, that as a result, she knew she could get killed anytime. I can appreciate her concern, for without being a social worker myself, I find life so dangerous and even in the peace of my present accommodation, I could not 100% agree that all will be well within a space of 24 hours. I say this with some remorse, for only last week, I was upset by a burglary of fine French furniture, which I wonder about. The Tory Government are not necessarily entitled to accept such fine objects at the expense necessarily of one's life. One hears of Aid workers working abroad in distressed areas of the world getting kidnapped for a possible cash for honours reward! What exactly the object of their betrayal to grand larceny me in this way will one day be told, maybe by the opponents who did it. This is all I say.

This identifies clearly what Isabelle de France was telling my father that day they lunched together at the Embassy residence in Westchester County. I suppose it is right to think that the murders happened on account of the lost 18th century French furniture of a few days previously. To aspire to using this for drugs is to clearly state how out of control the crisis of the drug war has become and how this is enditeable, as a result of it. I complain bitterly about this.

No, I doubt we are born equal and that we can equally share the social life be it you are underprivileged or at the other end of the social sphere as top people of the world. When I grew up I only met people like me. I was happier that way than I am now. My father introduced me to the best people socially speaking that anyone would wish to meet. As they say, in other words, one has to stick to one's own kind. While my father lived, I lived on the straight and narrow, and it never made me any unhappier than living another life which might be considered risqué or neglige. One finds one's own medium with life, and probably one can at least say, I am in complete control of it all. What other reason can be good enough?

Britain has recently fought a war against my country Japan. I am detained by the Court of Protection. Until discharge I will be held as a hostage, spied and watched upon.

Chapter 17 : An Art Gallery

My memory leads me to a small gallery in St James's where I once saw an exhibition from Hawaii of paintings in oil of angels wearing angels's wings and long robes, sitting at a café drinking cappuccino. They were generally angels and women with long hair. For some reason this memory never fades away, so I thought I would write about it. I knew a young girl who was oriental in looks who had beautiful long hair, slim and beautiful. She was meant to have a share of my father's money of course, but the real heirs never received anything other than a pittance like a coin thrown by Judas in that famous temple as a gesture of some point of recovery, if one can call such small sums of money something to actually appreciate! However, she lived in a youth hostel, for this is all she could find in the way of lodgings. Carolyn, who had become the great white cocaine and hard drugs dealer wanted her cappuccino, her whites outfit and her long hair, as well as Hawaii and exposed her to an overdose of heroin admitted intravenously by force into Elisa's arm, thereby killing her. This is something which prompts me to say that many of the angels came from a city of angels, and not necessarily Los Angeles, but from near that corner of the world. Elisa was from Hawaii, and I am sure I felt my mistake when re-entering the gallery, and told the exhibition had already been returned to Hawaii. One day, I will find one of them and buy it for the sake of this re-current memory of not very long ago, when Elisa was still alive!

The importance of this should not be ignored. After all as a small little girl, I passed through Honolulu and stayed with the Japanese couple and their daughter Wendy, who was the same age as me. He became a Senator, in Congress and was quite an important figure unto his own right, later on in life. So I could have returned to Hawaii. Elisa was around, a mole helping me in a case of some mal-function related to the communication with the children I had brought up, she was able to adjust something for them when and as necessary which I agreed with. I think Carolyn had her heart set on Tokyo and all that it stood for not only for me but the rest of the family, that she knew she must over-throw Elisa, in order to have even a half hearted attempt at gaining favour in the Pacific and especially my manager there of my company and the Michaels. I only mention this terrible story to prove that the former civil servants from the Court of Protection and Public Trustee's office were after my family members, who were often very poor, due to the means to deny them the money they sought to acquire from a family worth a lot in terms of money as well. They hooked them often on drugs to acquire payment for their regular "fixes" eventually leading to their miserable and unfortunate end. She already employs a standard and relied on prostitution and renting out sex to steal my family away from me.

These are cartoon days of the Ninja and the means to defy their prejudice and conspiracies as well. How to find out and gather information has been a battle of the warlord. It has cost a fortune!

There is much to fight about and becoming very space age. Like all Gallactic battles, there are injured and dead too amongst those encountering the battles to win their fortunes. For this I believe I have lived through certain

They plonked the ring onto the finger of their greedy Tai, and as it was a type of engagement ring to marry somebody I knew, they had by their act of robbery replaced that engagement for a destitute woman who made her living. By now, she is expecting his baby. She is a member of a terrorist organization and it was her organization that ended up killing a friend . She was fighting her boyfriend, another man, about the money again. She left him in miserable accommodation without heat light or running water, and I daresay he wanted to move into my home and have me leave it for him. He was accused as well of being a jewel thief working for the magpies. He was dragged away by their IRA women and their IRA executioner, a woman, cut him and there was a lot of blood on the floor as they "slashed" him. " Their Marl knew how to be intolerant to him and humiliated him in an outrageous manner fit for a terrorist.

Because of their very "sordid affair" I doubt myself she should have the baby but for the command of their IRA. I realize without their authority, there is nothing anybody can do about it. They want the baby to be an heir of mine. I am upset by this request for the sake of the counter measures used to get her accepted into the circle again. The unborn issue wants a guarantee of all my financial worth! How very disagreeable of them.

Otherwise, in the past he was my beau, the dark tall handsome man. He was seven years my senior and he never forgot how he was always teaching me as a young girl of 13. This was about the last time I saw him in New York. Now we "meet" again and I suppose old friends never really forget each other. Had I known he needed a place to live in by himself, and had I known the risk he was taking being with their Marl, I would have eagerly sought a way out of helping him. He always treated me for such a young girl and I'm sorry I didn't either understand better or he had not explained it clearly enough to me. I suppose I am to blame but I told him there were spare rooms and he could always stay in them if he so cared to. He never listened and ended up safeguarding me and looking after my second and younger grandchild Jordie, who he was positively so sweet and nice to. He saw to it that at least my son-in-law could come to fetch him but Jordie as usual went back to the wrong home.

He was my Official and Court for Italy and he gave me a long time visa to stay there and reside there. When the four Officials pounded their way in to claim "The Four Seasons" by Antonio Vivaldi, that is when I left Italy for good. The rest of them followed me back to London. I started making friends there. It's obvious that is not what the British wanted for me. And so I have related an important event which their Officials no doubt will remember me for, for good or for bad. The Italian case failed all. Diplomatically speaking it was not the ideal case or the ideal year from all points of view. Jordie's father was a Canadian from a Scottish ancestry. He died earlier this year or the end of last, leaving his two sons part of the time in the care of Helen. The mother is American. Jordie was a "great" child.

I wrote several books in 1987, which were lost and the various copies I held until 2006, were eventually stolen by someone who was interested in making money from them. The only short story out of five that can be called successful was "Sweet Possession" which underwent many episodes of robbery by thieves, interested for one reason or the other to acquire this book. It was written and finished in 1987. In 1987 I went to the South of France for a summer holiday, staying in my father's villa in Cap d'Antibes, the South of France. I had left my manuscips behind, but to my surprise, on top of my suitcase above my clothing I discovered my manuscript of "Sweet Possession. "There was the letter from Manchester Police attached to the documents. I then removed it from the suitcase and put it somewhere else in the room in the villa. Eventually I woke up one morning feeling unwell with a sore head. I thought I would go out. It was a very hot summer's day. I went into the next town being Juan-Les-Pins and due to the intense heat, was feeling dizzy and unwell. I went inside a new hotel near the Pinede (the main part of this small town) and sat down in the cool air conditioning. A receptionist approached me and asked me if I wanted to lie down and rest and was I feeling alright? I thanked her for her concern but insisted I did not need to hire a room and lie down yet. Maybe another time. She offered me something to drink. I asked her for a coca cola with ice. She sweetly went to get one and came straight back with a glass in her hand. I drank this down very quickly. I felt better. I realized later that my sore head was a result of an iron blow to my head, which kept the shutters of the French doors bolted at night. Michel Roccard, then Prime Minister of France took special care about my health after this incident and kept an eye on me.

At that time my Italian Policeman was working down in the South of France. Odd how I soon realized that it was a doctor who stole my manuscript and took it to a contact in Switzerland, a famous pharmaceutical company read it and it was sold for a great deal of money. For the cause celebre connected to this case, the doctor automatically acquired the whole of Juan-les-Pins, Antibes and Cap d'Antibes. I had no success in publishing this book ever, and though successful I must have lost the copyright to it sometime ago! The conclusion is that the doctor sold it for so much money to the famous pharmaceutical company, that by now, it is almost guaranteed I will always have a problem related to my copyright. However such things can be overcome. Of this I am certain. Whoever said crime doesn't pay? In this particular instance, nobody would say this for better or for worse.

The footballer's wife organized parties and set up a line against privacy for the "ripp off". She worked arranging these parties to get to know socially a lot of people. I was always excluded to their parties. I think it was their Carrow who socially excluded me for upheaval and an unlikely score like a "coup" against the social. In another words she wanted no meaningful rewards for me socially. It was a play for the antisocial to meet the social.

It was to be about the "Titantic" which hit an iceberg which shipwrecked all on board it for the catastrophe of a lifetime. When I first heard air-men saying after we had landed "it's all the tip of the ice-berg" I realized they meant that it was all for the "fall" of possibly the best. In my life, my memory cannot remember worse catastrophes happening socially to me by the deaths of my father , of my children, of friends and even a lover or two! I wish the rage for war could stop, but it's the "tip of the ice-berg" and we may know soon, possibly by Christmastime that another nuclear war may descend on us looming over the world like a terrible black cloud. This is irrelevant when speaking of religion and religious beliefs by the former Pm Tony Blair, who has forgotten his better manners of late. Most people would have preferred to remember that in public one does not normally talk out loud about "Politics, Religions and Money". But he may turn a blind eye to the questions

crying all the time and went home in a happier mood, and I returned in a better frame of mind, thinking quite openly that I had done a good job for my old ex hubbie.

Just before our return home, the last Sunday, I remember their Tom, married to Lucy , who lived in Ibiza Spain. They turned up at the Duomo with a contingency of Americans. Lucy and the baby had suddenly died. It was a case against their French public transport. Lucy was married to an American. The French neighbor gets very nervous about love going right for some as their public transport involvement brought no good to the happy little family. They should take care and watch what they do.

At home with Randy who looked after the Yorkie
Bonnie in New York State. 1989 approximately

This was a particularly surprising incident. It is marvelous how the Americans know how to find or look up their friends at a moments notice. I was pleased they came to Florence to go to the Duomo with a choir of American singers singing perfectly beautifully. It was an incident that took us by surprise!

Many years ago, during the time of the divorce between 1985 – 2001, I left my first Yorkshire terrier in the United States with Randy and his girl-friend. I had no money at the time and had returned to London. When Randy rang, he asked me for money to continue looking after Bonnie. I spoke to my former husband about this. All I asked for was about $100. He refused. A few days later, the dog ran out into the highway, and a passing truck ran over her and the dog died. Randy was heart-broken and phoned me to give me the news. Christopher could afford £100 as anybody could from England. His lack of concern and neglect is what probably caused the accident. We have never quite forgotten that side of Christopher either.

True, there has been a lot of sorrow in our lives of late. It is grief we must walk around with, like a perfume from days gone by.

In October 2006, after five years of having no holiday, I took time off to visit Istanbul, Venice and Florence. Shopping was fun but expensive. I purchased two rugs, plus an ottoman circular coffee table inlaid with mother of pearl, and an icon from Russia, which I must get back from a young sneak thief who substituted it for something else. I have some difficulty regarding my security with my front door, and it reminds me of years before, when Christopher then living with me used to refer to the Russians as people rushing in and rushing out, which made them RU.S.SIANS!

I live in a constant time zone of war and conflict because of their IRA.

Their vice and terror does not stop and the crime around me or my family can only make me conclude that those they defend are drug addicts who want my money, as substitutes for me for aid from the account. This is explaining her reason for not giving me back my father's Last Will and Testament. Their IRA Chinese authority tries to pretend superiority which normally damns me. I have no need of advice from a well known leader of their past such as the militant Chang kai Tchek. It happens to me because of the money my father left us as a family in Trust! Money is always the beginning of any crime.

Chapter 19

Now I will discuss the work of the U.N. peace mission. Japan did not enter the United Nations until 1956, and became a representative in the Security Council for the first time, in 1958. My father's prominence rose because of the case whereby he agreed with the United States Ambassador, Cabot Lodge, regarding the withdrawal of American troops from Lebanon, which became a case where the United Nations involved themselves under the influence of their argument, that a military intervention in a local war was wasteful and unnecessary. Cabot Lodge proposed that American military intervention be stopped. In a small local community where the various sects of Muslims, were squabbling about some local problem, he felt it was not worth worrying Congress to pay for American military to be present and in a land that was so far away, as well from the U.S.A.

It was later proposed that a U.N. police patrol be set up in cases where small and local trouble or war broke out, and from this fostered the idea of a U.N. peacekeeping mission. This meeting happened in 1958, and the first to agree with the American was my own father.

Japan had it's own Self Defense Forces. It was permitted under Article 51 of the Charter of the Un the right of individual or collective self-defense " inherent as a right of member countries. "

Article 5 of the San Francisco Peace Treaty and the pre-amble of the U.S.-Japan security Treaty which stated "Japan's provision of military bases to another country and jointly defending itself with that country has been correctly

will take Kosovo many years to return to the state of a land in peace rather than the trouble it was left in, by the Nato forces, whose brutality matched their strikes on that country. Many complained about this from Japan such as Mogami Toshiki .

"While proclaiming their activity "humanitarian Nato member countries did not rescue the victims of suffering, but punished the victimizer from afar instead, placing the safety of the reprisal force foremost, punishing, the victimizers can sometimes be effective, but one would think it was essentially more important to rescue the victims of oppression, even if it meant the rescuers had to expose themselves to some degree of danger. It is not easy for people to make such a self-sacrifice, it goes without saying. But it is impossible to just evade what has to be done and resort to violent means, facilely labeling them "humanitarian". Herein lies the fullest proof that the bombing of Yugoslavia was not what one would call humanitarian intervention. "

"One adds that the humanitarian intervention in Kosovo resulted in the concept of the end of geography. Tokyo felt no need to be involved in the struggle. European nations might have felt a security threat from the Kosovo conflict but would not have felt a security risk from IRAQ."

Sadakata Mamoru, a Japanese expert on former Yugoslavia made this comment" The problem with humanitarian intervention in the Kosovo crisis was that it was not truly carried out of humanitarian consideration. First of all "there was intervention" but it was the idea that it was humanitarian to justify it. For the U.S. it was not "non intervention of a humanitarian kind" nor was it a "humanitarian intervention" at all. At a meeting in Rambouillet, the U.S. demanded Nato deployment in

Yugoslavia or Nato airstrikes against their targets. This was "internal intervention" or "military intervention". But where Yugoslavia was concerned, it is clear nobody thought or considered at all. "

Joseph Nye of the U.S.A in 1999 said as follows:

1)The degree of Intervention should reflect the degree of concern and military intervention should be reserved for the most serious cases; 2) the use of force should be avoided unless both humanitarian and national interests are at stake;3)there should be a clear grasp of what is meant by genocide;4) great care should be taken when intervening in civil wars waged in the interests of national determination. "

"In the meantime, one remembers Article 1 of the U.N. charter which says that its purpose is to maintain "international peace and security. " The power of any permanent member of the Security can veto any resolution, proves that it is not at all completely fair or equal as an organization . For instance when China vetoed a motion to continue PKO activiety in Macedonia, that country fell into total civil war which is still fresh in the memory. China vetoed due to it's displeasure that Macedonia had tied up relationships with Taiwan. The U.N. malfunction is clearly evident in the War against IRAQ. "

"Political scientist Onuma Yasunaki states without prejudice that "international society will not tolerate human rights infringement on the scale of the German Holocausr even if the nation in question protests that such action involves intervention in its domestic affairs. Today no country no despot can ignore this principle. This is agreed in a general world movement. "

Japan is asked to remain a permanent member of the Security council but that it must "open a better vision for a wider range of U.N. reforms. "

The Japanese Diet, eventually agreed, after much deliberation since 1968, through to 2006, about the policing and mine sweeping abilities as well as their humanitarian aid objectives, to be an affordable offer. The cheque book policy wasn't very popular although $40million was contributed to aid Pakistan during the turmoil of the Afghan crisis, when the U.S. told Japan "to show the Japanese flag. "

In previous years, Japan's reply to the international conflict of the Gulf War and it's "trauma" in 1991, committed Japan to contributing to the international community in this particular crisis. This was the moment the sum of about $13billion was offered in that cheque book policy which at the time did not go down well.

However, by the later time of the other war in the Middle East and Afghanistan, the momentum rose again much to the satisfaction of the community in Pakistan. The failed cheque book policy made a swing about turn, and this became very much a policy of a "must" situation which became the symbol of the times and the mark of the war of terror.

Much of the time, there was a certain mis-understanding about their reason for being slow in reacting to the universal request to join in these wars and fights of lands thrown into disunity by the wars from the border and the country next door! Japan is an island and the character and temperament of the Japanese does not have conflicts such as those characterized in the western hemisphere. Besides this, Japan has no real direct neighbor as such, and difficulty to sympathize with the behavior of neighbor to neighbor borders were not placed high in a priority on the agenda of the Diet. I have quoted something here about this.

The other wars in Rwanda were acceptable wars of the worst order where internal hatred between two groups, namely the Hutus and the Tsutis erupted into a terrible conflict, where barbaric butchery was employed, reminding one of the inhumanity and barbarism of the internal war in Cambodia led by the Khymer Rouge. All these unsettled areas were policed and intervention was made, though not with great success due to the nature of the conflicts.

International Conflicts

"After the 9/11 attack in New York City a Security Council Resolution 1386 was drawn up implementing a unanimous cooperation and with urgency to bring "justice to the perpetrators, organizers and sponsors of this terrorist attack" 28 September 2001. Under Chapter V111 Charter of the United Nations resolution 1373, the state must legally feel the obligation to prevent "funding of terrorists and their acts , preventing movement of terrorists by effective border controls, and finding ways of intensifying and accelerating the exchange of operational information regarding actions of terrorists persons and networks". This was the implementation of resolutions by Japan in the post September 11 attack which included Chapter V111 an operation for peacekeeping OR peace-enforcement. "

In 1992, a review was set up to look at the PKO law and anti terrorism management law, dealing with the creation of a new Anti terrorism Bill and amendment of the PKO law, " to meet the demand from the changing climate of international security and of the crime's management system. " After September 11, a new Anti terrorism Bill was passed with the new and amended PKO law. President Koizumi asked his Cabinet Ministers to send if at all available, a league of SDF for counter- terrorist activities as

UNPCC

This Bill envisaged the creation of a U.N. peace cooperation corps which was to consist of non SDF employees, private citizens, direct subordinates to the President and members temporarily transferred from SDF. Proposed law specified activities of the corps and included overseeing ceasefire agreements, monitoring elections, medical activities, disaster relief of measures and transportation, telecommunications and other logistical support. The Government announced that the U.N.PCC members would be allowed to carry small firearms in order to defend themselves. This Bill however was abandoned due to lack of conviction by the Diet, general public and press as to it's validity for the sake of a constitution of the SDF. Contribution like a "cheque book policy" gave U.N. peacekeeping budget at the time of $13billion. This was too much as the budget for peacekeeping at the time amounted to $3billion! The government were forced to impose special taxes on their citizens to grant this contribution to the U.N.!

ANTI TERRORISM BILL

This rule covers activities such as providing supplies and services such as medical treatment to U.S. forces and their allies. It offers humanitarian relief to refugees with consent from the host governments. It allows search-and-rescue operations to provide for relief to those in need in areas declared in a critical state. This law is significantly different contrasting itself to the PKO law.

Under the PKO law, the SDF would be involved in operational areas where conflicts have ended, and the SDF, would be given activities for limited logistical missions, putting themselves in volatile areas, committed to universal objectives to save nations by sometimes using deployments to exterminate terrorists. Under PKO rule, the SDF would be allowed to use weapons for self-defense only. Anti – terrorism law would approve the use of weapons to protect those under SDF care including refugees and wounded foreign services members. In order to add flexibility to current and recurrent restrictions on the use of force, this law would have a two year time limit. This law would need Government consent to be allowed to dispatch SDF within 20 days. For this the law sought out Diet's approval.

Chapter 20

I conclude my book by saying that it has helped me to record the life of Dr Matsudaira my father and his career as a Japanese diplomat. I can only hope that it has helped others understand what it meant to be a representative of Japan in Russia, Paris, Ottawa Canada, New York and New Delhi in an era which was almost magnificent as far as the eye can see. He had vision, great charm, intelligence and understanding, far from the ridigity of today's world, with it's disciplinarians running the show much of the time! In his life, he offered me compassion. This is not something I receive much of anymore. This I believe is what most need and want in the world today. His name, Koto, meant peace of the east. Possibly we must try to have a clearer vision of the leaders we seek to find. Possibly in a small way, we can understand we would like more my father "Koto" and more those in the spirit of the Matsudairas. One of my relatives was a well known writer of Japanese literature, who wrote The Tale of Genji". This is a reason I picked up pen to paper and drew what I have written as a testament of my side of a family long in dispute with certain people concerning my life and finally my divorce, apparently a victim of "prostitutes" at the end of it all, well after his untimely death. My involvement with a man who kept secrets hidden for too long, lost us our future and our lives, and we will probably be separated for a long time to come. My father would have been the only one to patch it back together as he knew him and was fond of him. Otherwise, how would he have introduced me to him when I was so very young, a mere 12 or 13 year old? How could he have guessed that he never saw my father again after New York? In the meanwhile, the expressions both sides, for or against my father, have really shown some decency, and in spite of our differences. I think by writing this book, I may have succeeded in patching a few things up myself with the "on high" here in Britain, though it has cost more than life itself in terms of money. However the government have been sympathetic and tried to do what they could though they grappled in the dark having never met me. I wish I could know better how to deal with politicians and men in parliament, but maybe this will happen in the next life rather than in this one. Possibly I feel there is nothing to lose by not meeting certain people in Parliament, but this is not true, for my problems are so hateful, I could die as my only son just died yesterday, the 25. 08. 07 by a massive attack, so I am told. One never forgets their Queen of Jordan who said a mother was the most important figure of a family, more than a father, though the father is also important in a family unit. My observation so far is many men may not agree to this.

The Plan – December 2007

I realize that the IRA Marl, their Railway mother and her boyfriend will stop at nothing to be the "illegitimate" Matsudaira. It is their future plan for Japan now I speak of. Their new plan to defraud me is netting in all who I have known for sometime and a few friends. The new and stronger conspiracy unfolds, and I cannot say what more trouble I have to put up with from the Italian, whose mischief has settled any dispute with him personally about taking on a new love, for he generally sends in his doctor to quite take the pleasure away from me!

today. King Henry V did say as an opener to explain the part of the problem as a bachelor King "I cannot be King of England without being King of France". The war started, ending in victory for a British King who returned with a bride by his side. This is the suggestion, about those entitled to find their victory by the conquest of a beautiful girl for his bride! It does not suggest anything other than this. But this is Shakespeare and not unfortunately my ugly case. To conclude, JJ is from the Chinese side of my own Japanese family, whose family crest is Chinese, similar to my own. Her claim if it is at all true that she is from that Chinese family, which I have no proof of whatsoever, would be her entitlement to have influence about the family inheritance which is totally Japanese not Chinese. This is how the law is broken in an invalid claim with illegal practice trying to discredit me as a fraud no doubt! This must be the point of the exercise.

Once in Paris, a woman approached me saying that because I am beautiful, many people do not recognize who I am, for they believe I am too beautiful to be the true Matsudaira. I found this helpful in understanding my own personal problem here. However I agree the Receiver or Deputy as they now call themselves, behaves outrageously to me though he knows me well and who I am. I never heard of a solicitor trying to defraud their client so repeatedly as the many times he has tried it out on me. It must be something to complain about to their Office for Supervision of Solicitors in Leamington Spa!

I just gave in my clothes to be dry cleaned.

If they gave my clothes I sent in for dry cleaning to their JJ, no doubt, this is enough proof for them that she is in fact none other than me! This is the play they find accurate and solid as evidence in their ugly case against me for instance in a rip off to show if anything their undiluted scorn of me. For instance, JJ is very tall and a larger woman than me, however it may as well be just a simple case of jealousy laced with their true hate of me! JJ does talk very fast and gives the impression of moving in a smarter faster group than me. She is the Taiwanese mother of the girls. She wants money and be rich, proving her superiority all the time over one and all. She was in the same hotel as me in Genoa this past summer with her contingency of American people. She returned to London claiming my case, my identity and for the simple thrill of robbing me so I presume. She has enormous support. No wonder, I feel as if I am going through many battles of late. They are all Amina! It is Cruella all over again! Selfish hardened gold diggers on a repeat program to belittle and joke about me no doubt. They wanted to laugh all the way to my bank for it as before. She always claims destitution for a start, and has so far succeeded but this time it will not belong to the years of long ago when she was at her height as the prostitute and whore that seized France. She had innumerable children all girls! Indeed she has the backing of China and U.S. based CNN. A bit of bullying may go the right way for her, as the case reveals itself . I do not know if I shall be able to tell the reader how this case will end, as the book may have already gone into distribution by the time it is resolved.

As for the hostage

I do not like my life here as much as I should. I am spied and watched all the time. After all it was agreed so many years ago, that the Receivers of the past regime in Kingsway, London, would repeat the Prussian Revolution and the fate of Frederica, who experienced that Revolution together with her family in Prussia years ago. The civil servants wanted me to experience likewise and the same revolt as my fate like Frederica. It was always meant to be for her. This is a woman who together with her family, was forced to flee her country in haste, to seek freedom and life to live in the neighboring Republic of Germany. Had they remained in their castle, they would never have made it out alive, in all honesty! Frederica who never married, is an older lady, but who still works and lives here in London, together with her sister. They have moved here recently, within the past ten years. They have made their mark in the fashion world and in the drug traffic trade, remembering to take care of and be careful of my own health as a precaution, which shows certain manners of a better educated lady. I say this for a particular reason which I will not disclose in this book.

Consequently, as a mirror reflection of that time of great social upheaval, we look at the results of that time by way of the social revolution occurring in Britain today, forgetting "the former old England". The experimentation for blood has been severe of late, and barbarism in the butcheries of people has been the testament of their evil eye on the establishment to actually do little other than get rid of all of them. True, I think I speak here of a communist take-over in the Government, on one side of the coin. No doubt the present Government have a lot to cope with, without forgetting their place in the international community. There are fewer Americans and people from abroad now, unlike the past, and the general trend is over-powering in the condemnation and persecution of perfectly innocent people. Their mad really do run London like a force and deluge to bloody the streets once paved with gold! There is little to inspire international aid workers to help in the usual crisis. There isn't much to look forward to anymore, except windfalls from the banks upon the death of somebody like Princess Diana some years ago! Perhaps this is the long wait they seek, to remedy a supposed financial condition? Part of that reason is explained, but not all, for who can explain another problem caused by this revolution? Who can deliver us out of terrorism? How can I help by taking their medicine? I feel alone sometimes, and forebearing of their illicit desires for my wealth to procure for the sake and greater case of "illegal earnings". It could turn and become prostitution money if given over to her. Is this not communism at face value?

"The teacher may die"

On the news, there was an incident in Sudan, when a teacher was put into prison for naming a teddy bear Mohammad. She was accused of taking the Prophet Mohammad's name in vain. It was a most terrible accusation. She was a school teacher and from England. I phoned a friend who lives far away in Scotland. I explained how I considered the teacher completely innocent. I then told her about a case regarding a Mohammad, whose religious convictions was so intense regarding the birth of a baby boy from the Italian Luvi that it resulted in his committing a final sin which led to the unfortunate baby's case of misadventure or manslaughter. The infant never lived beyond a week or two of age.

Likewise, during the summer, without my being told a thing, my young infant daughter, was looked after by my maid. When I left for a summer holiday abroad, not intending to return for sometime, the maid gave my little girl to my security man, who is from a Muslim country. He had no idea what to do with the child. The worst happened, and the child was put into a bag into the rubbish for the

Chapter 21

Tokyo is far away and as stated earlier there is a case of drugged meat circulating which would place me in a questionable situation if I returned there. Coming from London, I could only make it a quick trip, and not a prolonged visit. I might commit a sin and tell more of my private problems. If I did I could only add on, the two different letters I wrote today to the Official Solicitor! But it is more "cost effective" to say that as a woman, in life, one has one's friends and one has one's lovers, who one has loved. It teaches us better the human condition and how to cope in a life that is far from splendid. However, one is left with fond memories which are more than I can say for many people in the world today. I will probably move on and probably love again, be it for better or for worse. Nobody will ever tell me that this is not allowed. In the distance, I can see Japan, but the slot is unavailable to me for the time being. The loss has been consequential. I cannot say how much older I shall be, when I die, but I never wanted to be placed in an old people's home for this is very inhumane. I am not old and I am not young. Some say I am beautiful. Others tell me how another is beautiful. I care not to change too much. It is better to go while life is still good. I believe in this firmly. The losses is what has made me resign myself to an end which I would never have dreamed of(, meaning the death of some of my children and baby sons and baby girl,) and I doubt it has given me over any more freedom than I had before for while they remained alive. True immigration to move to Europe is more strained than previously. This is what happens sometimes after the fall of members of the family.

I have my family cemetery in Japan, where I will probably be buried with the rest of my ancestors. It is sad to think most naturally that it becomes a case of the cemetery "from dust we are born". My daughter will visit my grave, as we had visited his grave on so many different occasions. He died in Tokyo aged 92 on the 4th May 1994. He left a daughter, being myself the writer of this book, and one grand-daughter and a couple of grand-children both boys. There were many people who attended his funeral and the Emperor of Japan, Akihito phoned my daughter personally in her hotel room to convey his condolences upon receiving the news of Dad's death. He was buried in our temple in the West of Japan, where we have our own private cemetery. A mausoleum was erected for him. He must be a well loved father and grand-father! The eastern sun shone brilliantly on his grave each year we visited his mausoleum! It almost seemed he was happy for our visit in the world beyond and made it a lovely day for us!

I leave you now at the end of my book with those words of fond memories.

THE END

Printed in the United Kingdom by
Lightning Source UK Ltd., Milton Keynes
142411UK00001B/74/P